the healthy southwest table

the healthy southwest table

janet e. taylor

RIO NUEVO PUBLISHERS

TUCSON, ARIZONA

Rio Nuevo Publishers®

P.O. Box 5250, Tucson, Arizona 85703-0250

(520) 623-9558, www.rionuevo.com

Text © 2007 by Janet E. Taylor. Photography © 2007 by Rio Nuevo Publishers.
Food styling by Tracy Vega. Many thanks to Deirdre and Scott Calhoun for the generous
use of their home for the photo shoot. Photography credits as follows:
W. Ross Humphreys: pages 11, 14, 17, 20, 23, 24, 27, 28, 35, 36, 41, 82, 87, 97, 126, 129, 145,
182, 186, 191, 192, 196, 200.
Robin Stancliff: front and back covers, pages 3, 6, 8, 9, 12, 13, 18, 31, 33, 34, 42, 53, 56, 59, 75,
89, 93, 98, 101, 113, 121, 122, 135, 147, 153, 155, 159, 164, 169, 170, 174, 178, 188, 205.
Katy Parks Wilson: pages 199, 203.

Library of Congress Cataloging-in-Publication Data

Taylor, Janet E.
The healthy southwest table / Janet E. Taylor.
    p. cm.
Includes index.
ISBN 978-1-933855-01-1
1. Cookery, American—Southwestern style. I. Title.
TX715.T2375 2007
641.5979—dc22
                    2007000022

Design: Karen Schober, Seattle, Washington.

Printed in Korea.

10   9   8   7   6   5   4   3   2   1

With much love I dedicate this book to my husband, Agustín, and our children, Elicia, Alex, Amanda, and Blake, for whom these recipes were created. And to our sons-in-law, Bobby and Ben, daughter-in-law, Kim, and our grandchildren, Ty and Aaron, who have joined us in laughter and the good times at our healthy table.

contents

Sit Down to Deliciously Healthy Food

If you dream of a healthier style of eating, *The Healthy Southwest Table* will make the transition deliciously palatable and sparked with south-of-the-border flavor. This eclectic collection of taste-tempting, low-saturated-fat recipes treats your taste buds to a savory adventure, from succulent Margarita Salmon with Fresh Fruit Salsa to mouthwatering Spinach Enchiladas and Black Bean Pasta Salad with Tangy Cilantro Sauce. These delicious recipes—derived from over thirty years of healthy cooking—are embellished with an array of foods containing potent substances that can strengthen the immune system and possibly protect against chronic illnesses such as cardiovascular disease, cancer, Alzheimer's disease, and diabetes.

These recipes were born of necessity, because three of our four children had elevated cholesterol levels at birth. We began to take control of our family's diet in 1974, the year our first child, Elicia, was born. Her pediatrician was participating in a research study involving cholesterol levels in newborns and alerted us that Elicia's cholesterol was higher than normal. Because of this, along with the fact that my husband's mother had died at age thirty-six from cardiovascular disease, the doctor cautioned us that what my husband and I did about Elicia's diet during early childhood would affect her cardiovascular health as an adult.

I realized we had to make lifestyle changes or face the consequences later; so without hesitation, we took his advice and set into motion a healthy lifestyle for our family, emphasizing diet and exercise. We started reading research studies and well-documented literature to learn what could be done to ensure a healthy cardiovascular system for our tiny little daughter, whose

future was in our hands. By the time we had three children potentially at risk for heart disease, we were doing our best to create a
healthy environment for our family. Our family's diet evolved
based on knowledge taken from valid research studies and author-
itative articles on diet and the prevention of chronic disease.

Although our children grew accustomed to eating sensibly
and enjoying the food prepared at home, we were not blind to
the possibility that they would not always eat the right foods—
yes, we knew they would indulge in junk food. Not being fanat-
ics, we figured if they ate properly at home, eating fast foods
and junk foods once in a while was not going to hurt them. Our
goal was for them to know what was healthful and to usually
make wise food choices. It paid off; three of our four children
have healthy blood cholesterol numbers today. As young adults,
they are all health-conscious eaters who consistently try to
make sensible food choices. However, due to his job, our son
Alex travels five days a week, living in hotels and eating all
meals away from home. He doesn't eat at fast food restaurants
and is very conscious of what he chooses from menus, including fish a couple of times each week. But his lifestyle is fast-
paced, with little rest and no exercise, and his cholesterol
numbers could be better.

We believe those lifestyle choices made years ago have given our
family a better chance of escaping not only cardiovascular disease,
but other diseases as well. Today Elicia, a healthy mother of two little boys, continues the tradition. Her sons get plenty of exercise and
enjoy a variety of foods in their health-promoting diet, which
includes recipes from this cookbook. Favorite recipes of her older
son, Ty, include Cranberry Soda and Spicy Spinach Pizza.

Encouraged by friends and family, I decided to write *The
Healthy Southwest Table*. Most of the recipes are Southwest-
oriented and contain many flavors from Southwestern and Mexican cuisines. My husband's Mexican heritage brought tortillas to
our table, so serving tofu, beans, poultry, fish, or meat seasoned

with salsa and wrapped in a corn or whole wheat flour tortilla seems natural for us. I also surmised from my reading that the traditional Mediterranean and Japanese diets seemed to be the healthiest in the world, so I based my family's diet on them, too.

Delicious food is one of the pleasures in life. These recipes were created with satisfying flavors, aromas, and textures in mind; and the most discerning of all critics did the testing—children and teenagers. If a dish was not tasty, they wouldn't eat it. We also had the perfect testing ground—our home. It often seemed more like a diner, with our children and their friends grabbing a bite to eat before going to play sports, going out for the evening, or just hanging out at our house. When I first began to write *The Healthy Southwest Table*, I had the food critics—the "kids"—rate the recipes on a scale of 1 to 10. Any recipe averaging below an "8" had to go back for improvement. *The Healthy Southwest Table* recipes have been tested by teenagers, our adult children and their friends, our three-year-old grandson, and family friends. Our friends were often pleasantly surprised to learn what was in the recipes they gave high scores.

Throughout the book I have included information based on research findings about foods and their preparation (see "Highlights of Some Nutritional Studies" and "Making Smart Food Choices" at the end of this book for more information). Did you know that fruits and vegetables contain powerful antioxidants such as vitamins C and E, and carotenoids that can build up your immune system and assist your body in disposing of cancer-causing agents? Are you aware that nutrients such as folate (also called folic acid) in many fruits, vegetables, and grains can transform potentially heart-damaging elements into harmless by-products, while others reduce naturally occurring, cell-damaging free radicals that put our bodies at risk for disease? Do you know that soy may contain substances that reduce the ills of menopause and may decrease the risks of osteoporosis and prostate cancer? Do you know that the manner in which you

prepare foods and some processes used by food manufacturers can increase your risk for disease? I've shared these phenomena with you so you can understand the design of the recipes and take more control of your own health through your diet.

Fortunately, many potent disease-fighting substances are in common foods available in your local grocery store, such as avocados, extra-virgin olive oil, nuts, soybeans, black beans, tangerines, cabbage, tomatoes, chiles, red peppers, grapes, papaya, strawberries, garlic, salmon, and flax, to mention just a few. Even so, many of us have difficulty including the required amounts in our family's diet on a regular basis—but not any more. *The Healthy Southwest Table* makes it easy by providing recipes containing health-promoting ingredients, so you can easily and frequently incorporate them into your diet.

The recipes follow recommendations from the American Institute for Cancer Research and the American Heart Association. And since being overweight is also a health hazard, the recipes provide a sensible approach to weight control. They are low in saturated fat, contain little or no refined sugars, and have little or no processed foods. To tantalize your palate, the dishes taste and look good. Therefore, it should be easy to shed a few unnecessary pounds, and the more these healthy recipes become a part of your daily diet, the easier it will be to achieve and maintain a healthy weight.

You too can take control! Let *The Healthy Southwest Table* assist you in preparing appetizing meals based on an array of health-promoting ingredients. These healthful recipes are bursting with lively and bold Southwest flavors to satisfy your palate. Enjoy good times around the dinner table with your family while providing them with healthy dietary habits that can have profound effects on their lives today and, even more so, in the years to come. With these recipes, you are making an investment in your family's health that will pay dividends well into the future.

What's on the Healthy Southwest Table?

In creating the recipes I focused on including fish and a variety of colorful fruits and vegetables, which will grace your table with lively festive appeal. Piquant chiles, roasted red bell peppers, cilantro, lime, Mexican spices, and a mélange of other colorful plant foods will bring a bouquet of earthy and boldly flavored Southwest flavors for your pleasure and your health. The components of the recipes include:

Vegetable dishes usually feature not just one, but a number of colorful vegetables mixed together to achieve a broader spectrum of phytonutrients (potent antioxidants that attack the free radicals in our bodies that cause disease). They are grilled, broiled, baked, or steamed to achieve a crisp yet tender texture and to retain more of their nutrients.

Beans are frequently used in combination with colorful vegetables. They are nutrient-dense and high in fiber.

Only whole grains are used. Pasta is used to accent dishes, not as a main ingredient.

Golden flaxseed ground into flaxmeal is included in recipes to boost beneficial Omega-3 essential fatty acids (EFAs).

Fish and chicken dishes usually don't stand alone but may include vegetables, nuts, seeds, and soy. Fish and chicken dishes are often accompanied by a salsa or sauce that is loaded with fruits or vegetables or both. If vegetables are not included in the recipe, a complementary recipe of fruits or vegetables is recommended. Fish and chicken are grilled, broiled, or baked. Moderate temperatures are used to retain Omega-3 EFAs. The first choices for fish are small wild Alaskan salmon and sable fish, which are high in Omega-3 EFAs and have less mercury than most other fish. Organic free-range chicken is suggested. Four-ounce servings are suggested for both fish and chicken.

Organic free-range eggs with Omega-3 EFAs are recommended due to a 3:1 ratio of Omega-6/Omega-3 and also the manner in which the chickens are raised.

Extra-virgin olive oil is used extensively. Moderate to low cooking temperatures are used to retain its healthy profile and not convert it into an unhealthy substance. Olive oil is frequently added after the recipe is cooked in order to retain its antioxidants. Unrefined macadamia oil is used in desserts in place of butter and in drinks to achieve a creamy texture. It is high in monounsaturated fat and has a healthy 1:1 ratio of Omega-6/Omega-3 EFAs.

Goats' milk yogurt and cheese, and some cows' milk cheese, are used in moderation.

Soy is used to reduce the amount of animal protein. Main dish recipes incorporating soy are substituted for meals containing meat to reduce the saturated fat in the diet. Soy is used in creating sauces or in soups, drinks, and desserts.

Trans fats such as margarine, shortening, and other hydrogenated oils are completely taboo.

I made a concerted effort to achieve an overall low glycemic load (GL) in each recipe or combination of recipes (see page 195).

The majority of recipes are naturally anti-inflammatory (see page 189).

Cooking Tools

COFFEE GRINDER. A coffee grinder with the blades close to the bottom of the container will grind spices perfectly. Krups coffee and spice grinder is a good choice for around $20.

MICROPLANE GRATER/ZESTER. This tool looks like a knife but with a large grating plane instead of a blade. It is the best tool for zesting citrus and grating hard cheeses. The cheese grates light and fluffy, so you use less. You can find one for about $15.

OIL PUMP SPRAYER. A stainless-steel container with a plastic lining that you partially fill with oil, screw on the spray cap, pump to pressurize, and then spray the oil. Use to spray on foods during grilling or in pans and skillets to prevent sticking.

VEGETABLE STEAMER. Available in bamboo, ceramic, and stainless steel. The steamer suspends the vegetables above boiling water, reducing the leaching of nutrients into the water. I prefer a bamboo steamer, with separate bamboo containers layered on top of each other, which allow for steaming various vegetables at the same time—or just one layer can be used. It can also be taken from the stovetop, placed atop a plate, and used as a serving dish.

Soy Products

Soy has become one of the most widely touted food sources in the twenty-first century. Soy offers a complete protein and can be substituted for meat or mixed with meat to reduce saturated fat. There has been much debate and research concerning the health benefits from using soy, and ongoing research continues to study its possible benefits in reducing the risks of heart disease and osteoporosis, and in boosting the immune system. Genistein (an isoflavone that has an estrogen-like effect on mammals and seems to inhibit or slow the growth of tumor cells), along with other beneficial components found in soy, may reduce the risk of hormone-related cancers, increase effectiveness of radiation therapy for prostate cancer, reduce PMS symptoms, and reduce hot flashes during menopause. Traditional Asian diets, which provide much higher soy consumption over the course of a lifetime than the typical U.S diet, seem to correlate with significantly lower rates of breast and prostate cancers.

Asians also eat whole soy foods, not the protein powders that have become so popular in the U.S. in recent decades. The less processed it is, the more benefits derive from soy; cooked dry soybeans, boiled edamame (fresh in the pod), soy flour, tempeh, miso, tofu, and soy beverages retain more isoflavones than foods such as soy cheeses, hot dogs, and bacon, and they also (with the exception of tofu, soy milk, and miso) add fiber to the diet. Unfortunately, soy food manufacturers do not list the amount of isoflavones contained in their products, but it is still important to read the labels. Some products contain unhealthy oils and large amounts of sugar. I also don't recommend using soy oil, which is approximately 60 percent polyunsaturated fat and is more susceptible to rancidity than olive oil or canola oil.

SOYBEANS are available dry, canned, fresh in the pod, and frozen in the pod. Dry soybeans can be cooked and included in a variety of recipes. They must be soaked for eight hours and cooked about four hours. The fresher they are, the less time they will need to cook. Canned soybeans, which come in black and yellow, are the easiest to use. Fresh or frozen soybeans in the pod (edamame) are easy to prepare: just add them to boiling water and cook until tender. They make a great snack or can be added to recipes. Buy soy foods made from organic soybeans, which have not been genetically modified. You will find edamame in the frozen vegetable section of the grocery store.

TOFU, available in regular and silken form, is usually found in the grocery store's produce section or cold case. Both types come in soft, firm, and extra-firm, and are available in low-fat varieties. Extra-firm and firm tofu have a higher protein content because they contain less water than the softer options. Soft regular tofu lends a creamy, smooth texture to dips and cream sauces. Soft silken tofu makes drinks and dips creamier than soft regular tofu. Firm regular tofu is used instead of cheese in cheesecake. Firm and extra-firm regular tofu are good for stir-fries and in salads where you want the tofu to hold together and have a firm texture. I don't recommend using firm or extra-firm silken tofu.

Tofu packed in an aseptic package (which has been sealed in a carton under sterile conditions) has a shelf life of approximately nine months and does not require refrigeration prior to opening. Regular tofu is usually packaged in a sealed tub container with water and needs to be refrigerated. Before using either kind, check the expiration date. Both may be used straight from the original packaging in recipes that require no cooking, such as dips and drinks. Once opened, both kinds of tofu must be stored in water and kept covered in the refrigerator; the water must be changed daily. Any tofu that is stored in the refrigerator after the package has been opened will need to be cooked before using in uncooked recipes, such as dips, to eliminate the possibility of harmful bacteria like salmonella. Immerse in boiling water and cook on low for 5 minutes. (If a recipe is cooked, the tofu does not have to be precooked.) Silken tofu will become mushy if boiled. It needs to be placed in boiling water and then allowed to cook below the boiling point.

If you want a crumbly, somewhat firm texture that resembles the texture of ground meat and will readily absorb marinades, you should freeze, thaw, and then drain the tofu; expel the excess water with your hands; and crumble. (Freeze only regular tofu; silken will become slushy.)

Tofu's protein and fat content varies according to the type (regular or silken) and the degree of firmness. It also varies by manufacturer. Check the labels. If you want high-protein tofu, extra-firm usually has the most—approximately 8–9 grams per 3-ounce serving.

SOY FLOUR is made from whole soybeans. Substitute ¼ cup of soy flour for ¼ cup whole wheat flour in baking bread, waffles, muffins, etc. Stir into soup or sauces to thicken. It does change the flavor, so you will have to experiment. Soy flour is available in the health-food section of most grocery stores.

TEXTURED VEGETABLE PROTEIN (TVP) is made from defatted soy flour that has been cooked under pressure and dried into granules. Pour boiling water over TVP and allow it to sit for 10 minutes to rehydrate. Mix with ground meat or use as a meat substitute. It is available in the health food section of most grocery stores.

MISO is fermented soybean paste and works well in sauces, soups, and dips. Use miso in place of salt. It should be added at the end of cooking to avoid pasteurization, which will destroy the beneficial enzymes. Mellow miso has less sodium than regular miso. Check the labels for sodium content, with a goal of keeping daily sodium to 6 grams. Miso is available at health food stores and Asian specialty stores in the cold case.

TAMARI (SOY SAUCE). Look for organic or "traditionally brewed," made by the ancient Japanese method of "koji" fermentation. Tamari does not contain wheat and is available in low-sodium varieties. Traditional organic shoyu is an alternative to tamari, but it contains wheat. Many soy sauces labeled as tamari or shoyu are defatted by a petroleum derivative and are artificially fermented. Eden Foods is one respected manufacturer of both soy sauces.

SOY BEVERAGES (also called **SOY MILK**) are available under numerous brand names. It's important to read the label to determine how much protein, fat, calcium, and sugar each contains. They are available in plain, vanilla, carob, cocoa, chocolate, and strawberry flavors. Soy drinks are also available in nonfat and low-fat versions. To achieve a creamy drink, many manufacturers have added canola oil or corn oil, which adds fat. Often there is also a trade-off between fat and sugar—you may have low-fat soy milk, but with sugar added for flavor. Sugar, rice syrup, high-fructose corn syrup, or other sweeteners are added to some soy drinks and may contribute 7 to 18 grams of additional sugar per 8-ounce serving. Drinking sweetened soy milk as a substitute for cow's milk is not a healthy choice. If you want a flavored soy milk, buy it unsweetened and add a small amount of stevia—the natural alternative to sugar—and fruit or cocoa, and blend it up. For a creamy texture, add unrefined macadamia oil, which is high in monounsaturated fat. Organic soy milk is recommended because it is made from soybeans that have not been genetically modified.

SOY CHEESE can be mixed with regular cheese to reduce saturated fat, or used as cheese by itself. Look for soy cheese that contains canola oil, which is high in monounsaturated fat. Soy-Sation, made with canola oil, has a good taste and is available in a 97-percent fat-free option. Soy cheese does not have as many of the health-promoting properties as the whole soy foods. We usually mix tofu with soy cheese to increase creaminess and isoflavones. Soy cheese is available in some grocery stores and in all health-oriented food stores.

In *The Healthy Southwest Table*, soy is often combined with chicken or used as the base for some soups, drinks, and desserts. It can be used to reduce saturated fat by reducing the amount of animal protein. Compared with other beans, soy has the highest amount of protein. It is better than other plant protein because it has all eight essential amino acids.

Additional Preferred Foods for the Southwest Table

As we stepped into the twenty-first century, many of the health-promoting foods used in this recipe book had started to find their way into grocery stores around the country. Many major grocery stores today have health-food sections. If you have difficulty locating a particular ingredient at your local grocer, try looking for it in a health-oriented grocery store or health food store.

AVOCADOS are used extensively in Mexican and Southwest cuisine. This creamy fruit is full of fiber, is a good source of vitamin E and folic acid (folate), and is about 70 percent monounsaturated fat. It contains the phytonutrient beta-sitosterol, believed to lower "bad" cholesterol (low-density lipoproteins, or LDL) while maintaining or increasing "good" cholesterol (high-density lipoproteins, or HDL). It also contains the phytonutrient glutathione, which neutralizes free radicals in our bodies, reducing the risk of chronic diseases. Haas avocados are the most flavorful and have the most monounsaturated fat. A ripe avocado will not be hard but ever so slightly soft and not shriveled. The art of cutting and peeling an avocado is to first cut a half-inch-wide slice, pop it away from the seed, then peel the section. The sections can be larger, but that is usually the individual serving size. Continue doing this until you have the entire avocado cut and peeled.

CHILES. CHIPOTLE CHILES are dried and smoked red jalapeños. They impart a woody, smoky flavor, can be extremely hot, and are used extensively in Southwest foods. GREEN CHILES are popular in Southwest cooking. Usually roasted and peeled, they vary in heat. New Mexico green chiles are usually hotter than Anaheim green chiles. JALAPEÑO PEPPERS range from green to red. They add heat and flavor and are widely used in Southwest foods. You can never predict how hot a jalapeño is going to be—like all other chiles, they vary in heat. POBLANO CHILE is an essential ingredient in Southwest cuisine. It is a flat, pointy-tipped, deep green chile about the size of a bell pepper. It has a very rich, full flavor with varying degrees of heat. Usually the poblano is chosen for chile rellenos. *The Healthy Southwest Table* uses it instead of green bell peppers.

The heat of the chile is in its veins and seeds, so if you want to eliminate some of the heat, remove them. However, you may lose some health-promoting benefits by doing so—benefits seem to be associated with capsaicin, which also gives chiles their heat. Capsaicin may lower triglycerides, LDL, and total cholesterol in the blood, making it heart-healthy, and it may reduce the risk of some cancers, speed up metabolism to help maintain a healthy weight, and reduce inflammation. Fresh green chiles are also abundant in vitamin C. As they turn red they lose some vitamin C but gain vitamin A. In addition, drying green chiles decreases vitamin C and increases vitamin A. Both vitamins are high in antioxidants, which kill off free radicals in our bodies, reducing the risk of disease. Vitamin A is also known as the anti-aging vitamin and for building up the immune system. Medical research has delved into the medicinal powers of chile through scientific studies, which have included clinical trials. Most fresh chiles are available in the produce section of most grocery stores. Dried chiles are usually found in the Mexican food section.

COUSCOUS is a form of pasta made from the heart of durum wheat that has been finely ground. These recipes use whole-grain couscous in order to reap the most benefits. The bran and the germ are still intact in whole wheat, providing a source of high-quality vitamin E (an antioxidant), fiber, iron, B vitamins, and many other nutrients. Whole-wheat couscous is usually found with the pasta, rice, and other grain products in the grocery store.

EGGS. Omega-3 organic free-range eggs have a 1:3 ratio of Omega-6/Omega-3 and are increasingly available in most grocery stores. A diet with a balanced Omega-6/Omega-3 ratio is part of a disease-preventive diet. Organic free-range chickens are also raised in a healthier, more humane environment.

FISH. Some fish contain more harmful pollutants than others, and their consumption may need to be limited or avoided completely. Small, wild red sockeye salmon from the Pacific Northwest are known to have the least amount of pollutants. Oceansalive.org posts advisories on pollutants in fish and how much is safe to consume. Since different types of fish may contain different pollutants, it is also safer to eat a combination of fish during a week to avoid the same contaminants.

FLAX PRODUCTS. FLAXSEEDS are tiny, shiny seeds having a milk-chocolate or golden color with a pleasing, nutty flavor. Among plants, these are the richest source of Omega-3 essential fatty acids (alpha-linolenic acid) and are a rich source of the antioxidant vitamin E. They are also high in fiber. Golden flaxseed has more of a nutty, buttery flavor than brown flaxseed. Both usually have the same amount of Omega-3 essential fatty acids. However, in order to obtain their health-promoting substances, they must be ground into FLAXMEAL OR FLAXSEED MEAL, or chewed extremely well to break the seeds and allow the oil to escape. Otherwise, the seeds will remain intact and pass through the digestive system without providing any value from the oil. Flaxmeal is produced by grinding flaxseeds in a blender or coffee grinder. In order to retain the nutrients after grinding, refrigerate in an airtight container. Grind only what you will use within a couple of weeks. FLAX OIL, such as Spectrum Essentials organic flax oil with cinnamon, is an excellent source of Omega-3. Add to smoothies for creaminess and cinnamon flavor. It may also be consumed by itself.

GINGER (CRYSTALLIZED, CANDIED). Ginger is known to reduce inflammation. Spicy-sweet crystallized ginger is made from fresh ginger root that is candied and coated with cane sugar. One or two cubes will nicely sweeten smoothies and other drinks. Crystallized ginger contains sugar, so use sparingly; fresh ginger root is a better option for frequent use. The spicy-hot ginger flavor makes a tasty complement to many foods. Experiment by finely grating fresh ginger and adding to fish, salads, and vegetables. Your taste buds will enjoy it, and your body will benefit from its properties.

GOAT CHEESE AND YOGURT are easier to digest than those made from cow's milk. Unlike cow's milk, goat milk is not homogenized. During homogenization, fat globules are mechanically broken, freeing xanthine oxidase to later penetrate the intestinal wall. Once in the bloodstream, this enzyme can cause scarring of the heart and arteries, which may stimulate the release of cholesterol into the blood to cover the scarred areas with a protective fatty material. Many individuals with dairy allergies can eat foods made from goat milk. Unlike cows, most goats are raised without growth hormones and are allowed to graze naturally rather than be confined to stalls in massive milk-production plants. Goat cheeses are becoming readily available in many grocery stores, and most health-oriented grocery stores carry them.

HERBS AND SPICES, used as flavor enhancers in cooking, also have disease-fighting properties. *The Healthy Southwest Table* advocates generous use of herbs in flavoring recipes to provide a variety of phytochemicals that protect against chronic diseases. Since basil, oregano, rosemary, citrus peel, cilantro, chives, garlic, mint, and parsley are easily obtainable fresh, I have frequently made them a part of the recipes. They contain heart-healthy and cancer-fighting phytochemicals; for example, citrus peel (which contains the phytochemical limonene) may assist the liver in ridding the body of cancer-causing substances. Oregano is the best source of rosmarinic acid, an antioxidant with anti-inflammatory and antibacterial properties; basil and cilantro also provide rosmarinic acid. Rosemary, known as the remembrance herb, may contain compounds that help fight Alzheimer's disease. Most of these herbs are easy to grow and impart a delightful taste to many foods.

MACADAMIA NUT BUTTER, is high in monounsaturated fat and is anti-inflammatory. You can find it in health-oriented and gourmet grocery stores; as its popularity increases, it is also increasingly found in major grocery chains.

MACADAMIA OIL has a healthy fat profile of 78 percent monounsaturated fat, 14 percent saturated, and 7 percent polyunsaturated, with a 1:1 ratio of Omega-6/Omega-3 EFAs. Unrefined, expeller-pressed or cold-pressed macadamia oil is used in desserts in place of butter and in drinks to achieve a creamy texture. It is available in health-oriented and gourmet grocery stores, and, due to the popularity of the Hamptons Diet, it is becoming more available in major grocery chains.

MAPLE SYRUP, when used in these recipes, should be 100 percent pure maple syrup; read the labels.

NUTS AND SEEDS. To preserve the health benefits of nuts and seeds, they should be eaten raw. When used in cooking, low to moderate temperatures are recommended. PECANS are often used in Southwest cuisine and are grown in Georgia, Texas, New Mexico, Oklahoma, and Arizona. Among nuts, pecans, walnuts, and hazelnuts rank highest in antioxidant load. Pecans are 60 percent monounsaturated fat, 30 percent polyunsaturated fat, and only 10 percent saturated fat. Rich in fiber, they make an excellent source of vitamin E (in the form of gamma tocopherol) and contain natural plant sterols, which have cholesterol-lowering abilities. Pecans should be stored in the refrigerator or freezer to maintain their nutritive values. At normal temperatures, pecans out of the shells retain their freshness and largely unoxidized state for about three months; however, all nuts should be kept in the refrigerator or freezer to maintain their freshness and avoid rancidity. PIÑONS OR PINE NUTS are frequently used in various diets of the Mediterranean people, have been a staple for the Navajo, Apache, Hopi, and many other tribes, and, for centuries, have been a part of the cuisine of what is now Mexico. Piñons are also often used in modern Southwestern cooking. Like all nuts, they are high in calories and should be used primarily as a garnish, as in so many of the Mediterranean dishes. A few go a long way. Piñons have a high concentration of monounsaturated fat and polyunsaturated fat and are a good source of thiamine, potassium, magnesium, zinc, copper, and dietary fiber. PISTACHIOS, depending on their origin, have a percentage of monounsaturated fat between 52 and 74 percent, and the polyunsaturated fats vary between 16 and 35 percent. They are an excellent source of antioxidants and fiber. Since they are calorie dense due to their fat content, they should be eaten as a garnish. A few nuts are heart healthy! PUMPKIN SEEDS or PEPITAS, which are hulled seeds from a variety of squash, have a lower fat content than piñons and nuts and are a good source of monounsaturated and polyunsaturated fats. They have been used throughout the ages in Mexican sauces. They are available in health food stores and in most grocery stores in the same area as nuts or in the health food section of the store.

OLIVE OIL, which is approximately 75 percent monounsaturated fat and 15 percent saturated fat, also has 9 percent Omega-6 EFAs and 1 percent Omega-3 essential fatty acids (EFAs); compared with other common oils it has the highest content of monounsaturated fat and the lowest in Omega-6, making it the most neutral oil as far as Omega-6 and Omega-3 EFAs are concerned (see page 202 for more on EFAs). It also contains high-quality vitamin E and health-promoting polyphenols; polyphenols have been shown to increase HDL and to limit production of LDL. Most other common cooking oils don't have polyphenols, so olive oil is most often recommended in this recipe book. The level of polyphenols differs according to where the olives are grown; extra-virgin Tuscan olive oil boasts the highest level. The polyphenol hydroxytyrosol, known for its anti-inflammatory properties, may be what has kept people healthy on the island of Crete. Hydroxytyrosol has a peppery bite, which you will feel at the back of your throat when you swallow a teaspoon of olive oil. Extra-virgin olive oil is produced from the first, unrefined pressing of the olive. The least processed olive oil and olives may reduce the risk of many chronic diseases. Extra-virgin olive oil should be used at low to moderate temperatures in sautés and no more than 350 degrees Fahrenheit in the oven. It should be stored in the refrigerator to prevent rancidity.

PAPAYA. When choosing a papaya, look for one that's golden orange on the outside with tiny speckles of green. It may have some spots that look a little too ripe or even some moldy spots, which are okay. Never buy one that is green. Wash the outside of the papaya with a vegetable wash, then dry with a paper towel. Papayas have an abundance of vitamin C and are good for digestion.

PICKLED PLUM PASTE is a salty, reddish paste made from the Japanese umeboshi plum. It is pickled in salt and shiso leaves. It gives blended tofu a sour cream- or yogurt-like flavor and creates a nice substitute for them. It also adds salt to recipes. It will change a recipe from bland to tasty. It is available in the Asian food section of most grocery stores or health-oriented grocery stores.

PORTOBELLO MUSHROOMS are large (3–7 inches in diameter) mushrooms. They provide a meat-like texture in recipes. They are available in most grocery stores year-round.

QUINOA (pronounced keen-wah) is a complete-protein grain from South America. It supplies all of the essential amino acids in a balanced form. It is available in health-oriented grocery stores and the health food sections of most major grocery stores. **QUINOA PASTA** is usually made from whole-grain quinoa in combination with other non-gluten grains. It is available in health-oriented grocery stores.

SALMON, WILD ALASKAN SOCKEYE. Wild salmon is the richest food source of astaxanthin, a powerful antioxidant that also gives wild salmon its color. Astaxanthin is believed to reduce inflammation and to have positive effects on the cardiovascular and immune systems. Sockeye salmon has the highest amount of Omega-3 of any fish and is one of the least contaminated by mercury. In 2005, the *New York Times* exposed a number of markets as selling farmed salmon for wild salmon—at the higher price of wild salmon! Farmed salmon are often administered antibiotics and are substantially higher in saturated fat and lower in Omega-3 than wild Alaskan sockeye salmon. Farmed salmon have also been found to have higher levels of toxins than wild salmon. During the winter months, wild salmon is not generally caught. Therefore, beware! Often, fish labeled "wild" is not. Your best bet is to buy frozen wild salmon during the winter and fresh wild salmon during the spring and summer.

SALSA. If you use bottled salsa, look for healthy salsa that has a limited amount of salt, no sugar, and no vegetable oils (a little olive oil would be okay).

STEVIA EXTRACT is an extremely sweet, noncaloric herb. It is available in liquid or powder form and is available in health-oriented grocery stores. It is sold as a supplement, not as a sweetener. A scant amount of powdered stevia extract, $\frac{1}{40}$ of a teaspoon, is all that is needed for sweetening (it may help if you think of this as a tenth of $\frac{1}{4}$ teaspoon). If you use too much, it will impart a bitter taste. Since stevia is available in a number of different forms—liquid, powder, powder plus fiber—follow the package directions for use. You might need to experiment to determine the quantity needed.

TOMATOES (CANNED). Choose canned tomatoes consisting of tomatoes, tomato juice, salt or no salt, citric acid and calcium chloride. Organic is recommended. The whole tomato—skin and all—delivers the most health benefits. Tomatoes are loaded with lycopene, which has potent antioxidant properties that help to neutralize harmful free radicals in our bodies. Cooked tomatoes deliver about five times more lycopene than fresh, because cooking frees the lycopene from the cell walls of the tomatoes, allowing it to be easily absorbed through our digestive systems. In Mediterranean cuisines, tomato sauces are often cooked for hours. Thus, canned tomatoes—even though they are peeled— are a healthy option for a quick meal.

TORTILLAS. When buying tortillas, it is important to check the label. CORN TORTILLA ingredients should be corn, lime, and salt, and Trader Joe's carries an organic corn tortilla made from just that. Don't buy those containing wheat, oil, or chemical additives and preservatives. There are two types of corn tortillas: *gordita*, meaning "fat" in Spanish, and the thin tortilla. *Gorditas* are more flavorful and do not harden as fast as the thinner variety. They are available from local *tortillerias*, many of which supply local grocery stores. FLOUR TORTILLAS should always be made from whole grain or, better yet, sprouted grain. (The traditional flour tortilla is made with lard and white flour.) I prefer Food for Life Ezekiel 4:9 organic sprouted whole-grain tortillas. Labeled "diabetic friendly," they have been clinically proven to be low-glycemic (meaning they have the least possible effect on blood sugar levels). They are available in health-oriented grocery stores. Many manufacturers today use shortening or canola oil, and a few use olive oil. There are also red chile, jalapeño, and sun-dried tomato tortillas. HEMP TORTILLAS from Healthy Hemp are tasty. They are difficult to roll but are good for tostadas, for serving with soup, or to scoop up beans. Gluten free, low in carbohydrates, high in fiber, they contain 10g protein, 8g fiber, 2g net carbohydrates, and are high in Omegas 3, 6, and 9 with a ratio of Omega-6/Omega-3 of 2:1. Visit www.healthyhemp.com to find a retailer near you.

TUNA is an excellent source of Omega-3 EFAs and protein and is low in saturated fat. Check for mercury levels at oceansalive.com. Vital Choice packs young, sushi-grade albacore tuna that has been line-caught. This tuna has about one-third the amount of mercury compared to standard tuna. You can shop at vitalchoice.com.

WHOLE GRAINS. Products containing white flour or even unbleached flour just don't cut it in a disease-prevention diet. They have been stripped almost entirely of fiber, protein, and naturally occurring vitamins B and E. Yet look around you—most breads on grocers' and bakeries' shelves are white, unbleached, or only partially whole grain. Pastas are usually not made from whole-grain flour, and most rice is white. Then there are the quick-cook oats and other quick-fix cereals, which are not completely whole grain. According to the American Heart Association, Americans consume about half the fiber needed for a heart-healthy diet. Coupled with a low-saturated-fat diet, 25–30 grams of fiber from foods (not supplements) are essential each day to lower the risk of heart disease. Fiber-rich foods—whole grains, legumes, vegetables, and fruits—can reduce cholesterol. Fiber reduces the absorption of fat consumed in the diet. It is not only beneficial to the heart, but is one of the factors necessary in preventing other diseases, including many types of cancer.

Recommended Brand-Name Ingredients

ALVARADO STREET SPROUTED PIZZA BREAD contains organic sprouted whole wheat berries, organic unbleached white flour, filtered water, wheat gluten, safflower oil, honey, fresh yeast, salt, cultured wheat, olive oil, and bread crumbs. Visit www.alvaradostreetbakery.com to find a retailer near you.

ARIZONA CACTUS RANCH PRICKLY PEAR NECTAR is 99 percent prickly pear juice and pulp with no sugar added. There is some indication that prickly pear products promote cardiovascular health. Visit www.arizonacactusranch.com to order products.

ARIZONA'S FINEST CHIPOTLE BBQ SAUCE contains tomato puree, distilled vinegar, sugar, salt, raisin paste, chipotle peppers, crushed orange puree, spices and herbs, dried garlic, corn starch, xanthan gum, potassium sorbate, and caramel color. It makes barbecue sauce a little more exciting by imparting that bold, earthy, smoky flavor with a bit of fire, distinctive of the chipotle chile. It is available in grocery stores in the Southwest and on the manufacturer's website, www.arizonafinestfoods.com.

CHERI'S PRICKLY PEAR CACTUS SYRUP is made from fruit harvested from prickly pear cactus in the southern Arizona desert. This syrup will add sugar, so it should be used sparingly. A teaspoon with lemon and naturally carbonated mineral water is mighty tasty, with a beautiful fuchsia color. It is available in many grocery stores in the Southwest, or visit www.cheris desertharvest.com to order products.

MACNUT is a brand of macadamia oil (see page 24). It is available in health-oriented grocery and health food stores.

MORI-NU SILKEN-STYLE TOFU, packaged in convenient 12-ounce aseptic packages, is available in organic form; buy organic since the majority of non-organic soybeans are genetically modified. Visit www.morinu.com to find a retailer near you.

NASOYA TOFU is available in a 16-ounce vacuum-packed tub of water. Visit www.nasoya.com to find a retailer near you.

REDWOOD HILL FARM supplies yogurt and cheese from free-range goats devoid of antibiotics, growth hormones, GMOs (genetically modified organisms), or toxic pesticides.

Organic Foods

The U.S. Department of Agriculture has implemented national standards for food labeled "organic," whether it is grown in the United States or imported. Organic meat, poultry, eggs, and dairy products come from animals that have been raised free of antibiotics and growth hormones. Organic food is produced without the use of most conventional pesticides, fertilizers made with synthetic ingredients or sewage sludge, bioengineering, or ionizing radiation. For food to be labeled "100 percent organic," all ingredients, with the exception of water and salt, have to be organically produced. Products labeled "organic" must contain 95 percent organically grown ingredients, with the exception of salt and water. Five percent of the ingredients may consist of nonagricultural substances approved on the national list or agricultural products not commercially available in organic form. Organic produce is often more expensive than non-organic produce. According to the Environmental Working Group website (http://ewg.org), the twelve most contaminated non-organic produce items are apples, bell peppers, celery, cherries, imported grapes, nectarines, peaches, pears, potatoes, red raspberries, spinach, and strawberries. They are referred to as the "Dirty Dozen." Daily consumption of these may result in exposure to approximately twenty pesticides. The twelve least contaminated are asparagus, avocados, bananas, broccoli, cauliflower, corn (sweet), kiwi, mangos, onions, papaya, pineapples, and peas (sweet). These foods contain only two pesticides. As a healthy option, buy organic produce for those classified as most contaminated and nonorganic for those classified as least contaminated.

Recommended Brand-Name
Ingredients, continued

ROSARITA ENCHILADA SAUCE, available in many grocery stores, is made with canola oil, which is an important factor in choosing this brand. **HATCH ENCHILADA SAUCE** is also good.

SANTA CRUZ CHIPOTLE PASTE is produced in Tumacacori, Arizona. There are 2g of sugar and 5g of carbohydrates per ¼ cup. Use paste in lieu of boiling and pureeing your own dried chipotle peppers. Visit www.santacruzchili.com to order products.

SPECTRUM NATURALS makes great-tasting spreads that don't contain the potentially harmful oils found in most margarines.

Also see "Tortillas" on page 28.

A How-To for Roasting, Toasting,
Grilling, and Working with Tortillas

Basic Roasting Techniques for Vegetables and Portobello Mushrooms

Roasting vegetables brings out or develops their flavor while preserving nutrients and retaining the freshness and firmness of the flesh. Fire-roasted chiles and tomatoes, in particular, are essentials in creating bold flavors and fragrant Southwest cuisine. You can roast vegetables under the broiler of your oven, on a gas or electric grill, or over charcoal. The open-flame method imparts a smoky flavor—especially if roasted over charcoal or wood chips. Broiling, however, is most efficient when you are pressed for time. Since grilling vegetables varies a little, each vegetable is listed here with specific details. Some vegetables require a little oil before and during roasting, while others are often not oiled until after cooking (this retains more of the health-promoting properties of the oil).

For most vegetables, the broiler or electric or gas grill will be set at high heat. Once it is hot, place the vegetables on a broiler pan and put it under the broiler as close to the heat as possible. If using a grill, place vegetables on the grill. If you are using a barbecue grill, place whole peppers or tomatoes or other prepared vegetables on the grill over hot coals, but not in direct contact with the flame. Broil or grill the vegetables, turning as they blister. A slight browning and grill markings on the vegetables add visual appeal. Some vegetables are grilled over moderate heat, which is indicated in their grilling instructions. Be careful not to burn the flesh. To retain a firm texture, allow the skin to cook quickly so the meat of the vegetable is only slightly cooked. If you want shish kabobs, tomatoes, bell peppers, onions, and summer squash all take about the same time to grill and can be grilled together on skewers.

Charred vegetables do not have the same risk of containing cancer-promoting elements (such as heterocyclic amines, or HCAs, and polycyclic aromatic hydrocarbons, or PAHs) as charred meat, poultry, and fish. Both HCAs and PAHs are created from fat dripping into the coals, which then permeates the food through smoke and flare-ups of the fire. Therefore, it may be good practice to grill the vegetables before the meat to prevent the vegetables from soaking up PAHs and HCAs.

CHILES, BELL PEPPERS, AND TOMATOES. Grilling peppers and tomatoes is slightly different from grilling other vegetables. If they are to be used in a recipe or stuffed, they are blistered and charred rather than slightly browned. Chiles and bell peppers should be roasted whole and peeled after roasting, as the tough peel often has a bitter flavor. I usually don't peel tomatoes but leave the charred skins to add color to the sauces and add more of a roasted flavor. If used on skewers with other vegetables such as summer squash and onions, peppers and tomatoes are not charred and peeled but cooked following the squash-roasting instructions.

Using high heat, place the peppers and tomatoes on a broiler pan as close to the heat as possible, or if using a grill, place on the grill. Turn the peppers or tomatoes as they blister and blacken, being careful not to burn the flesh. To retain a firm texture, allow the skin to cook quickly so the meat of the vegetables is only slightly cooked.

Some people prefer to wear gloves while working with hot chiles, because the capsaicin burns their hands. Once the peppers are blistered and blackened, place them in a bowl and cover with a plate to allow all of the skin to release from each pepper. Since they will continue to cook, remove from the bowl as soon as the skins have released. Allow the peppers to cool. Don't place in water or run water over roasted peppers, or some of the oils and flavor will be lost. Peel the skins off the peppers and remove the seeds and veins. If you like hot peppers, leave some of the veins intact. If you are roasting peppers that are going to be stuffed, make only a small incision from the stem to about 1 inch from the tip of the chile. After peeling hot chiles, wash your hands thoroughly because the heat (capsaicin) will remain on your hands. I have more than once gotten chile in my eyes from my hands, and it does burn! If chiles are threaded on skewers with other vegetables, they are not blackened and peeled.

CORN is one of the easiest vegetables to grill or broil. As the corn cooks, some of the kernels will brown. As this occurs, turn the corn; continue to do so until some of the kernels are browned on all sides of the corn. The specks of brown on yellow or white kernels add aesthetic appeal to recipes. Remove from the heat and either serve whole or cut the kernels from the corn and add to salads, beans, etc. If eating corn on the cob, spray it with olive oil instead of smothering it in butter.

EGGPLANT. Slice the eggplant into scant ¼-inch slices and lay on a cookie sheet. Brush or spray both sides with olive oil and sprinkle lightly with salt. Allow to sit for 30 minutes before grilling or broiling. Grill or broil at a lower temperature or not as close to the broiler. If cooked at a high temperature, the pieces tend to burn before they are done. Remove from heat when the pieces are somewhat translucent and a little tender. Transfer to a bowl and cover. They will continue to cook slightly. If the eggplant is not going to be used in another recipe, add a little olive oil, minced garlic or garlic power, and salt and pepper.

GARLIC. Set the unpeeled garlic bulb on the grill or under the broiler. The skin will turn brown and be somewhat burned. Turn the bulb to assure even cooking. Depending on the method of roasting, this may take anywhere from 8 to 15 minutes. If you are roasting only garlic, use the dry roast method, which imparts more of a nutty, full flavor. Separate the cloves from the bulb. Don't peel. Place them in a heavy skillet over low to medium-low heat. Roast for 20–30 minutes, turning every 5 minutes or so to assure even cooking and browning. Whichever method you use, the cooked garlic will be soft. Peel and add to recipes. It can be refrigerated in a covered dish or plastic bag for a couple of days.

ONIONS. When onions are grilled, some of the strong flavor is toned down and the sweetness comes out. Peel and cut into ½-inch slices. Follow the basic grilling or broiling instructions, but don't blacken. They will appear slightly translucent and have a crisp, yet tender texture.

PORTOBELLO MUSHROOMS. Trim ½ inch from the tip of each stem. Slice the mushrooms ½ inch (or less) thick and spray or brush lightly with a little bit of olive oil. Sprinkle lightly with salt and pepper. Preheat broiler or grill to high heat. Arrange slices on broiler pan, not touching each other. Position broiler pan on top oven rack and broil for about 2 minutes or until the mushrooms are sizzling and turning a bit golden. Turn and repeat on other side. They should be tender yet firm.

SWEET POTATOES OR GARNET YAMS. The deep, rich color of the garnet yams and their texture make them my favorite of the two. Cut the sweet potato or yam into ¼-inch slices. Since it is a very dense root vegetable, it needs to be steamed prior to grilling in order to prevent it from burning before it is fully cooked. In a vegetable steamer, steam the slices for about 5 minutes or until they start to lose their firmness. Brush or spray lightly with olive oil. Grill or broil at medium high heat for about 5 minutes on each side or until they can be penetrated with a fork. The garnet yams will turn a deeper orange when cooked. Transfer to a bowl and cover. They will continue to cook a bit. They taste great without any added oil or seasoning. However, a few squirts of lime juice and a sprinkling of New Mexico red chile pepper powder adds some excitement—test one slice with chile pepper to determine the desired amount of heat.

ZUCCHINI AND YELLOW SQUASH. Depending on the size of the squash, vertically cut it into fourths or eighths. Broil or grill until crisp yet tender according to the basic grilling instructions, but don't blacken them. Transfer to a bowl and cover. They will continue to cook a bit. If the squash is not going to be added to a recipe, brush or spray with olive oil, and sprinkle lightly with salt and fresh, coarsely ground pepper.

Toasting Dried Chiles, Herbs, and Seeds, and Making Dried Citrus Zest

DRIED CHILES. The purpose of toasting dried chiles is to release the perfume captured in the chile, creating a full, bold flavor. Be cautious while working with the chiles. You may choose to wear gloves, but don't touch your eyes or lips! Make sure to wash your hands thoroughly after working with chiles.

Remove the stem and hard cap at the base of the stem. Open up the chile and shake out the seeds, removing the remaining seeds with your fingers. Separate or tear the chile apart to remove most of the seeds, for they are often hiding within little folds of the chile. If you can see the veins, you might want to carefully remove some of them, making sure that you're not throwing away a lot of the chile.

There are varying degrees of drying especially with the chipotle; you might get a chipotle that is moist or one that is really dry. The dryer ones are an earthy brown and have a very fragrant, smoky aroma, whereas the softer ones are red in color and have the texture of a soft sun-dried tomato. I like the brown type better.

Place a small heavy skillet over medium heat. Put the torn chile into the skillet. Be careful not to burn them, which can happen very quickly, or they will become bitter and will have to be discarded. When you start smelling the aroma of the chipotle, they are toasted. Remove from the burner and the skillet to prevent the chiles from burning.

TOASTING SEEDS AND NUTS. Place a small, heavy skillet over medium heat. When the perfume of the seeds is released and the seeds become slightly darkened—not browned—remove from the burner and from the skillet to prevent them from burning. Cumin and coriander seeds are often toasted and ground for Southwest recipes.

TOASTING DRIED HERB LEAVES. Place a small heavy skillet over medium heat. When the perfume of the herb is released and the leaves are darkening slightly around the edges—not browned—remove from the burner and skillet to prevent burning.

DRYING CITRUS ZEST. Preheat the oven to 225 degrees F. Into an oven-safe dish or pan, grate the zest from the citrus, avoiding the white pulp just under the skin. Place the pan on the middle rack of the oven and dry the zest for 20–25 minutes or until dry but not brown. Allow to cool. It may be stored in an airtight container in the refrigerator for about three weeks.

Broiling, Grilling, and Baking Fish and Chicken

When broiling or grilling fish or chicken, use a high temperature and cook very quickly to lock in the flavors. Bake fish and chicken at no more than 350 degrees F. Often olive oil is used in baking and grilling. Baking fish (or vegetables) in parchment paper retains all the juices and flavors and preserves most of the nutritional value. Aside from contributing to a healthy form of cooking, parchment paper also makes cleanup a lot easier.

Heating, Rolling, and Folding Tortillas

Tortillas have to be pliable in order to be rolled without breaking. There are a number of methods to accomplish this. If you are using a gas stove, place the tortilla over the burner with a medium flame. Turn the tortilla a few times until it is heated and pliable—not hard. Remove from burner, fill, and roll or fold. If you are using an electric stove, place a griddle or heavy iron skillet over a large burner and turn to high heat. When hot, place the tortilla directly on the uncoated griddle or skillet. Turn a couple of times until the tortilla is heated and pliable—not hard. Remove from heat, fill, and roll or fold.

CHAPTER

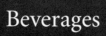

Beverages

South-of-the-Border Fresh Papaya Slush

(UNDER 30 MINUTES)
SERVES 3

2 cups cubed papaya

¼ cup Key lime juice

¼ cup maple syrup,
or substitute with ¹⁄₄₀
teaspoon stevia
extract powder

3–4 cups crushed ice

Calories per serving: 112
Total fat: 0g
Saturated fat: 0g
Calories from fat: 2
Protein: 1g
Carbohydrates: 29g
Dietary fiber: 2g
Sugars: 22g

Mexico is well known for its wonderfully refreshing fruit drinks. During our travels in southern Mexico, we loved the refreshing papaya drinks made with just papaya, lime, ice, and sugar—what a treat! Papaya is one of the healthiest foods available. It's extremely rich in carotenoids and is one of the best sources of vitamin C. Choosing the right papaya is important; see page 26 for tips to help you make a tasty selection. If you use maple syrup to sweeten this slush, check the label to make sure it is 100 percent pure maple syrup; or you can replace the maple syrup with stevia extract to reduce the glycemic load.

Wash the outside of the papaya with a vegetable wash. Cut the papaya in half and scoop out the seeds and stringy flesh. Cut a 1-inch slice off one papaya half, peel, and cut into pieces; repeat with the other half.

Place the papaya, lime juice, and maple syrup or stevia in the blender, and blend. Add ice and blend, turning the blender on and off to mix all the ingredients and create a fine icy slush. You may need to break up the mixture a couple of times with a spoon or dinner knife, but make sure the blender is turned off. Taste as you go. You should be able to taste the lime.

Desert Smoothie

(UNDER 30 MINUTES)
SERVES 2

½ cup **Mori-Nu soft silken tofu, or organic firm tofu,** drained

⅔ cup **Edensoy Extra Original organic soy milk**

¼ cup **Key lime juice**

1 tablespoon **Arizona Cactus Ranch Prickly Pear Cactus Nectar**

1–2 cubes **crystallized ginger**

1 tablespoon **unrefined macadamia oil** (optional)

2 cups **mixture of frozen mango, pineapple, and papaya**

Stevia extract powder (optional)

Calories per serving: 173

Total fat: 1g

Saturated fat: 0g

Calories from fat: 27

Protein: 7g

Carbohydrates: 32g

Dietary fiber: 3g

Sugars: 30g

This drink is our family's favorite. Ginger, which makes it even more tasty and satisfying, also has anti-inflammatory benefits. We have often gathered—very carefully—the prickly pear fruit from our yard and used its juice in this drink and other recipes.

One goal of a health-oriented diet is to limit the amount of sugar; therefore, try using a scant amount of stevia extract for sweetening. Only a trace—¹⁄₄₀ teaspoon of powder—should be used per 8-ounce beverage to deliver a pleasant sweetness (too much will cause a bitter taste).

Edensoy Extra soy milk is recommended due to its creamy texture. It is also fortified with calcium and other nutrients. For the creaminess and taste of ice cream, add macadamia oil. You will be adding fat, but it is about 80 percent monounsaturated and has a heart-healthy 1:1 ratio of Omega-6/Omega-3.

Place tofu, soy milk, lime juice, prickly pear cactus nectar, ginger, and macadamia oil (if using) in the blender and blend until smooth. Add the frozen fruit a little at a time.

As the drink thickens, you may have to stir (turn off the blender when stirring) and blend until the mixture is a smooth puree. Adjust thickness by adding more soy milk or break up the fruit, allow it to thaw a bit, and then blend some more.

Mangos are very sweet and usually add enough sweetness to the drink. Do not add more than 2 pieces of ginger; it will mask the fruit flavors. If more sweetness is desired, add a scant amount of stevia extract.

Macadamia oil increases calories by 60, calories from fat by 60, fat by 7g, and saturated fat by 1g per serving.

Variation—Blueberry Mango Smoothie

(UNDER 30 MINUTES)
SERVES 2

Calories per serving: 166
Total fat: 2g
Saturated fat: 0g
Calories from fat: 30
Protein: 8g
Carbohydrates: 28g
Dietary fiber: 3g
Sugars: 21g

Compared to all other fruits and vegetables, blueberries are nature's number-one source for antioxidants. Prepare this smoothie using the same ingredients and instructions as the Desert Smoothie but with the following changes: Instead of the mixture of mango, pineapple, and papaya, use 1 cup frozen blueberries and 1 cup frozen mangos; eliminate lime juice and cactus nectar; and the stevia is probably unnecessary. Instead of the optional macadamia oil, use an optional tablespoon of Spectrum Essentials organic flax oil with cinnamon, found in health-oriented grocery stores. The combination is really tasty, and by adding the flax oil, you are getting a good dose of Omega-3 EFAs.

Cinnamon flax oil increases calories by 60, calories from fat by 60, fat by 7g, and saturated fat by 1g per serving.

Variation—Strawberry Smoothie

(UNDER 30 MINUTES)
SERVES 2

Calories per serving: 177
Total fat: 2g
Saturated fat: 0g
Calories from fat: 29
Protein: 8g
Carbohydrates: 29g
Dietary fiber: 6g
Sugars: 16g

Prepare using the same ingredients and instructions as in the Desert Smoothie but with the following changes: For the fruit, use 2 cups frozen strawberries; eliminate lime juice, ginger, cactus nectar, and macadamia oil. Add 1 medium-sized banana for thickening and sweetness. If more sweetness is desired, add a scant amount of stevia extract.

Variation—Orange Dream Smoothie

(UNDER 30 MINUTES)
SERVES 2

Calories per serving: 177
Total fat: 2g
Saturated fat: 0g
Calories from fat: 29
Protein: 8g
Carbohydrates: 30g
Dietary fiber: 4g
Sugars: 23g

When you taste this smoothie, Dreamsicles might come to mind, with that wonderful combination of orange sherbet and vanilla ice cream. In advance, freeze 4 cups sweet tangerine sections ("honey" tangerine, aka Murcott mandarin). Prepare using the same ingredients and instructions as in the Desert Smoothie but eliminate lime juice, ginger, and cactus nectar. After blending the tofu and soy milk, add the frozen tangerine sections and blend until smooth. For a sweeter drink, add ¼ cup frozen pineapple pieces and ¼ cup banana slices or a couple of tablespoons of frozen orange juice concentrate, and blend. One tablespoon of unrefined macadamia oil can also be blended in for creaminess and to create a nutty flavor.

Macadamia oil increases calories by 60, calories from fat by 60, fat by 7g, and saturated fat by 1g per serving.

Cinnamon Hot Chocolate

(UNDER 30 MINUTES)
SERVES 4

**4 cups Edensoy Extra
Original organic soy milk**

**4–6 tablespoons unprocessed
cocoa powder**

**4 tablespoons maple syrup,
or ¼₀ teaspoon
stevia extract powder**

**½ teaspoon ground
cinnamon**

**4 cinnamon sticks,
for garnish**

Calories per serving: 198
Total fat: 6g
Saturated fat: 1g
Calories from fat: 49
Protein: 13g
Carbohydrates: 30g
Dietary fiber: 6g
Sugars: 13g

When you are in control of the ingredients in hot chocolate, it can be a healthy drink—just go easy on the sugar. The cocoa bean contains powerful flavanols that can act as antioxidants in the body, producing a positive impact on cardiovascular health. For the highest antioxidant content, choose cocoa derived from raw, unprocessed cocoa beans, which contain the most flavanols (don't use Dutch-process beans). Navitas Naturals raw cocoa powder is a good option and is available in health-oriented grocery stores and online.

Process all ingredients, except the cinnamon sticks, in a blender. Transfer to a medium-sized saucepan and heat over medium heat. Serve hot and garnish with a cinnamon stick.

Watermelon Cooler

(UNDER 30 MINUTES)
SERVES 4

**4 cups chopped
seedless watermelon**

3 tablespoons Key lime juice

Ice cubes

4 Key lime slices

Calories per serving: 49
Total fat: 0g
Saturated fat: 0g
Calories from fat: 2
Protein: 1g
Carbohydrates: 13g
Dietary fiber: 1g
Sugars: 10g

Agua de sandía *is a popular drink in Mexico, made of watermelon, water, and sugar. Undiluted sweet watermelon with a little lime doesn't need sugar, though, and it is ever so refreshing! Watermelon is rich in the antioxidant lycopene and poses potential health benefits due to its antioxidant content. Watermelon is also fat free and contains vitamins A, B6, C, and thiamin.*

In a blender, blend the watermelon and lime juice until the watermelon has liquefied. Pour over ice cubes in individual glasses and decorate with a lime slice on the edge of the glass.

Watermelon Cream Cooler

(UNDER 30 MINUTES)
SERVES 4

**3 cups chopped
seedless watermelon**

3 tablespoons Key lime juice

**1 cup Edensoy Extra Original
organic soy milk**

Stevia extract powder (optional)

Calories per serving: 69
Total fat: 1g
Saturated fat: 0g
Calories from fat: 11
Protein: 3g
Carbohydrates: 13g
Dietary fiber: 1g
Sugars: 8g

Inspired by the flavor and texture of watermelon paletas, *or ice pops, we have enjoyed in Mexico, I thought a creamy watermelon drink might be yummy. Thus, the Watermelon Cream Cooler came about. Edensoy Extra soy milk was perfect in providing just enough creaminess and flavor.*

Watermelon has an abundance of lycopene, and the fat in the soy milk increases the absorption of this powerful antioxidant. For a sweeter drink, add a scant amount of stevia extract, which has no calories and no glycemic load. Just $\frac{1}{40}$ teaspoon of powder is recommended per 8-ounce serving.

Place all of the ingredients in a blender and blend until the watermelon has liquefied. If desired, add a scant amount of stevia extract.

Creamy Fruit Shake

(UNDER 30 MINUTES)
SERVES 4

2 cups chopped
seedless watermelon

1 cup Edensoy Extra Original
organic soy milk

1 cup frozen strawberries

1 cup frozen mangos

1 tablespoon unrefined
macadamia oil

1 tablespoon organic
golden flaxseed

2–4 teaspoons organic
raw cocoa nibs

Calories per serving: 135
Total fat: 6g
Saturated fat: 1g
Calories from fat: 49
Protein: 4g
Carbohydrates: 20g
Dietary fiber: 3g
Sugars: 13g

This might sound like an unlikely concoction, but it is delicious and full of heart-healthy flavanoids, which contain disease-preventive properties. The fat derived from the macadamia butter, flaxmeal, soy, and raw cocoa enables the body to increase the absorption of lycopene in the bloodstream; this powerful antioxidant is generously available in the watermelon. Edensoy Extra soy milk is recommended because it is somewhat creamy, has a very pleasant taste, and is fortified with calcium and other nutrients. You can adjust the sweetness by using more or less mango.

Put all ingredients in a blender and blend until the fruit is slushy and flaxseeds are completely ground. Serve immediately. If the drink sits for any length of time, separation will occur.

Green Tea Cooler

(UNDER 30 MINUTES)
SERVES 4

4 green tea bags

4 cups water, divided

4 ounces unsweetened cranberry juice, not from concentrate

Stevia extract powder (optional)

Chopped mango (optional)

Calories per serving: 29
Total fat: 0g
Saturated fat: 0g
Calories from fat: 1
Protein: 0g
Carbohydrates: 8g
Dietary fiber: 0g
Sugars: 8g

Green tea may have powerful antioxidant properties far greater than those found in vitamins C and E. Research studies continue to explore green tea's disease-preventing characteristics.

Brew 2 cups of tea using 4 tea bags. Add cranberry juice and 2 more cups of water. If sweetening is needed, sweeten with ¹⁄₄₀ teaspoon of stevia extract powder per serving, or a few pieces of fresh, sweet mango. Pour over ice and serve.

White Tea Cocktail

(UNDER 30 MINUTES)
SERVES 4

4 cups brewed white tea

1–2 teaspoons Arizona Cactus Ranch Prickly Pear Nectar

1–2 frozen mango chunks, for sweetness

Calories per serving: 0
Total fat: 0g
Saturated fat: 0g
Calories from fat: 0
Protein: 0g
Carbohydrates: 0g
Dietary fiber: 0g
Sugars: 0g

Prickly pear cactus harvested from the southern Arizona desert adds flavor to white tea (the least processed of all teas, with a high level of natural antioxidants known as polyphenols) and may have heart-healthy benefits. The mango will infuse a tiny bit of sugar and flavor into the beverage, and since it is an excellent source of vitamins A and C, beta carotene, and fiber, the mango is a better choice than cane sugar. If you are having difficulty weaning yourself off sugar, try adding a scant amount of stevia extract for sweetness.

Mix all the ingredients together and pour over ice.

Red Rooibos Tea

(UNDER 30 MINUTES)
SERVES 2

4 rooibos tea bags

2 cups water

1 teaspoon lemon or lime juice

Stevia extract powder (optional)

Calories per serving: 1
Total fat: 0g
Saturated fat: 0g
Calories from fat: 0
Protein: 0g
Carbohydrates: 1g
Dietary fiber: 0g
Sugars: 0g

Caffeine-free red rooibos tea has a significant antioxidant capacity. It is a healthy drink for both children and adults.

Brew 2 cups of rooibos tea using 4 tea bags. Add lemon or lime juice, and if necessary, sweeten with ¹⁄₄₀ teaspoon of stevia extract per serving. Serve either hot or cold.

Cactus Soda

(UNDER 30 MINUTES)
SERVES 2

2 tablespoons Arizona Cactus Ranch Prickly Pear Nectar

24 ounces natural sparkling mineral water

Ice cubes

Calories per serving: 0
Total fat: 0g
Saturated fat: 0g
Calories from fat: 0
Protein: 0g
Carbohydrates: 0g
Dietary fiber: 0g
Sugars: 0g

We always tried to limit the amount of sugar our children consumed as they were growing up. Soda, being the American drink of choice, was usually available and offered to them at their friends' houses, and most soda is made with high-fructose corn syrup. An alternative is refreshing fruit soda that can be made at home with any type of unsweetened juice and sparkling mineral water; I like to use Italian sparkling water, but there are others as well. Adults and children will enjoy the bubbly with just a hint of flavor. Cactus soda has a beautiful magenta color.

Stir together the prickly pear nectar and sparkling water and pour over ice.

Pomegranate Soda

(UNDER 30 MINUTES)
SERVES 2

½ cup unsweetened
pomegranate juice

24 ounces natural sparkling
mineral water

Ice cubes

Calories per serving: 35
Total fat: 0g
Saturated fat: 0g
Calories from fat: 0
Protein: 0g
Carbohydrates: 9g
Dietary fiber: 0g
Sugar: 8g

Pomegranate is full of antioxidants.

Stir together the pomegranate juice and sparkling water and pour over ice.

Cranberry Soda

(UNDER 30 MINUTES)
SERVES2

¼ cup cranberry juice blend
without added sugar

24 ounces natural sparkling
mineral water

Ice cubes

Calories per serving: 37
Total fat: 0g
Saturated fat: 0g
Calories from fat: 0
Protein: 0g
Carbohydrates: 9g
Sugars: 8g

This is our grandson Ty's favorite soda. He's three and usually has an 8-ounce serving, so if you're serving small children, make the necessary serving size adjustments. Fruit juice should always be watered down, for both children and adults. It contains a lot of natural sugars, which enter the bloodstream rapidly.

Stir together the cranberry juice and sparkling water, and pour over ice.

Lime Soda

(UNDER 30 MINUTES)
SERVES 2

2 tablespoons Key lime juice

24 ounces natural sparkling mineral water

Ice cubes

Calories per serving: 3
Total fat: 0g
Saturated fat: 0g
Calories from fat: 0
Protein: 0g
Carbohydrates: 1g
Dietary fiber: 0g
Sugars: 0g

There is nothing more refreshing than lime in sparkling water. Limes contain flavanols, which protect cells against cancer. They are also packed with vitamin C, a powerful antioxidant that reduces inflammation, is heart healthy, and builds up the immune system.

Stir together the lime juice and sparkling water and pour over ice.

4

CHAPTER

Dips, Salsas, Sauces, and Rubs

Chipotle Creamy Dip

(UNDER 30 MINUTES)
MAKES 1¾ CUPS

1⅓ cups Mori-Nu
firm silken tofu, drained

1 clove garlic, chopped

¼ cup chèvre goat cheese

1 teaspoon Dijon-style mustard

2 teaspoons umeboshi
pickled plum paste

2 tablespoons Key lime juice

1–2 teaspoons Chipotle-Lime
Rub (see page 70)

2 tablespoons cilantro leaves

Calories per serving
(1 tablespoon): 12
Total fat: <1g
Saturated fat: <1g
Calories from fat: 6
Protein: 1g
Carbohydrates: <1g
Dietary fiber: 0g
Sugars: 0g

If you like garlic dip with a little bit of a kick, this one is for you. It's the perfect complement for a tray of fresh vegetables—which are full of insoluble fiber and rich in vitamins and minerals, a much wiser option than chips or crackers. Since flavors and textures are not compromised, no one will ever guess that this delicious dip consists mostly of tofu. A small amount of creamy chèvre goat cheese imparts a mild and delicious flavor and creaminess. It is similar to cream cheese but contains only a third of the fat and calories. Pickled plum paste is an essential ingredient that changes the flavor of tofu from bland to exciting. Although this takes less than 30 minutes to prepare, it should be allowed to sit for an hour before serving.

In a blender or food processor, blend all the ingredients until smooth. The amount of Chipotle-Lime Rub used will determine the heat.

Remove from blender, pour into a serving dish, and refrigerate for at least 1 hour to develop the flavors. If eaten immediately, there may be a strong garlicky bite. Stir before serving.

Basic Hummus

(UNDER 30 MINUTES)
MAKES 1¾ CUPS

1 can (15 ounces) garbanzo beans, drained (reserve broth)

1–2 tablespoons organic raw tahini (sesame seed paste)

3 tablespoons lemon juice, adjust to taste

1–2 large garlic cloves, adjust to taste

¼ teaspoon ground cumin

Salt

Calories per serving
(1 tablespoon): 31

Total fat: 1g

Saturated fat: 0g

Calories from fat: 10

Protein: 1g

Carbohydrates: 4g

Dietary fiber: 1g

Sugars: 0g

Hummus is a traditional dish in Greece, many other Mediterranean countries, parts of the Middle East, and India. Since not all garlic has the same strength, taste the hummus as you make it. Individual tastes also vary in the degree of tahini and lemon flavors preferred. Therefore, keep adding lemon and tahini until you have achieved the desired blend. Garbanzo beans are a good source of folate (folic acid) and contain a good amount of fiber—both are heart healthy. The sesamin in sesame seeds has been found to lower inflammation and cholesterol. Hummus goes Southwest in a number of tasty variations. Make the Basic Hummus and add the flavors of your choice, as suggested in the recipes that follow. Serve with a tray of colorful raw vegetables, such as broccoli, summer squash, peppers, cauliflower, carrots, or cherry tomatoes.

Place all the ingredients in a blender and blend until smooth, adjusting the lemon juice and garlic to taste. A little of the reserved bean broth may need to be added to achieve the desired consistency.

Green Chile Hummus

(UNDER 30 MINUTES)
MAKES 2 CUPS

1 Basic Hummus recipe (see page 58)

¼ cup roasted Anaheim or New Mexico green chiles (see roasting instructions, pages 34–36), or use canned green chiles

Calories per serving
(1 tablespoon): 28
Total fat: 1g
Saturated fat: 0g
Calories from fat: 9
Protein: 1g
Carbohydrates: 4g
Dietary fiber: 1g
Sugars: 0g

In the Southwest, we embrace the aroma of roasting chiles. Add some to the Basic Hummus for a spicy kick. To retain the crunch and flavor of the chiles, they are folded into the hummus rather than blended.

Roast the chiles while you prepare the Basic Hummus recipe to save time, then mince the roasted chiles. Remove Basic Hummus from blender and gently mix in the green chiles.

Chipotle Hummus

(UNDER 30 MINUTES)

MAKES 1¾ CUPS

1 Basic Hummus recipe, prepared without the salt (see page 58)

1–2 teaspoons Chipotle-Lime Rub (see page 70)

OR REPLACE CHIPOTLE-LIME RUB WITH THE FOLLOWING INGREDIENTS:

½ dry chipotle pepper

¼ teaspoon oregano

¼ teaspoon ground coriander

1 tablespoon chopped yellow onion

Salt

Calories per serving
(1 tablespoon): 31

Total fat: 1g
Saturated fat: 0g
Calories from fat: 10
Protein: 1g
Carbohydrates: 4g
Dietary fiber: 1g
Sugars: 0g

Chipotle Hummus makes a definite statement with its bold flavor. It will save time if you have the Chipotle-Lime Rub already made.

If using the Chipotle-Lime Rub, add it to the Basic Hummus and mix.

If not using the rub, toast the chipotle pepper and the oregano (see toasting instructions, page 39). Toasting releases the perfume of the chipotle and spices, rendering a wonderful bouquet of flavors. Remove the seeds and veins and break up the dry chipotle pepper. Add desired amount to the Basic Hummus recipe and blend thoroughly. Since chipotles are hot, try a small amount and then add to desired taste. Blend in the oregano, coriander, onion, and salt.

Pour mixture into a serving dish. Allow mixture to rest for 1–2 hours for flavors to thoroughly blend.

Cilantro Hummus

(UNDER 30 MINUTES)
MAKES 2 CUPS

**1 Basic Hummus
recipe (see page 58)**

¼ cup cilantro leaves

**1 tablespoon finely chopped,
seeded, and deveined
jalapeño pepper**

Calories per serving
(1 tablespoon): 28

Total fat: 1g

Saturated fat: 0g

Calories from fat: 10

Protein: 1g

Carbohydrates: 4g

Dietary fiber: 1g

Sugars: 0g

The citrusy flavor of cilantro complements spicy foods and goes well with beans, which makes it the perfect herb for hummus and jalapeños. It is not only an essential ingredient for many Southwest dishes, but it is also used extensively in both Mediterranean and Asian cuisines.

Using a blender, add the cilantro to the Basic Hummus and blend. Place the mixture in a serving dish, and stir in the jalapeños.

Roasted Red Bell Pepper Hummus

(UNDER 30 MINUTES)
MAKES 3 CUPS

1 **Basic Hummus recipe, prepared without the bean juice (see page 58)**

2 **large red bell peppers, roasted (see pages 34–36)**

1 **tablespoon minced fresh oregano leaves, or ½ teaspoon dried oregano**

1 **teaspoon turmeric**

¼ **cup pitted Kalamata olives**

1 **tablespoon extra-virgin olive oil**

Salt

Calories per serving (1 tablespoon): 23

Total fat: 1g

Saturated fat: 0g

Calories from fat: 10

Protein: 1g

Carbohydrates: 4g

Dietary fiber: 1g

Sugars: 0g

The flavors of roasted red bell peppers are a complement to the basic flavor of hummus. Turmeric adds a golden color, but most importantly, it reduces inflammation. Any time an ingredient that reduces inflammation can be added to a dish without compromising the flavor and presentation, it is a plus for your health. To be time-efficient, roast the red bell peppers while making the Basic Hummus. When preparing the Basic Hummus, don't add the bean juice. The red bell peppers will add liquid.

Add the red bell pepper to the Basic Hummus, and if using dried oregano leaves, add at this time with the turmeric, olives, olive oil, and salt. Blend until smooth. If using fresh oregano leaves, remove the hummus mixture from the blender and fold in the oregano by hand.

Traditional Guacamole Dip

(UNDER 30 MINUTES)
MAKES 2 CUPS

3 Hass avocados, sliced and peeled (retain the seeds)

2 teaspoons (or more) finely chopped fresh jalapeño pepper

2 Roma tomatoes, chopped

¾ cup finely chopped onion

½ cup chopped cilantro leaves

2 garlic cloves, pressed through garlic press

3 tablespoons Key lime juice

Salt and freshly ground black pepper

Calories per serving (1 tablespoon): 40

Total fat: 3g

Saturated fat: 0g

Calories from fat: 28

Protein: 1g

Carbohydrates: 3g

Dietary fiber: 2g

Sugars: 0g

Guacamole, great for dipping with corn chips, also makes a tasty topping for beans, chicken, and fish. The avocado is mostly monounsaturated fat, which has been associated with reducing cholesterol and inflammation.

With a masher or fork, coarsely mash the avocados in a medium-sized bowl and combine with all other ingredients. Put the seeds into the guacamole to keep it from turning brown.

Fresh Salsa

(UNDER 30 MINUTES)
MAKES 1¾ CUPS

1 cup finely chopped
salad tomatoes

1 medium-size jalapeño,
finely chopped

2–3 tablespoons minced onion

1–2 teaspoons minced garlic

½ cup minced
cilantro or basil

1 tablespoon olive oil

Pinch of sea salt

Freshly ground pepper

2 tablespoons Key lime juice

Calories per serving
(¼ cup): 24

Total fat: 2g

Saturated fat: 0g

Calories from fat: 18

Protein: 0g

Carbohydrates: 2g

Dietary fiber: 1g

Sugar: 1g

Fresh salsa adds enjoyable spicy flavor and a touch of color to fish, beans, poultry, and meats. Also, where there is color, you have phytonutrients. For the best flavor and texture, eat within a few hours; it can, however, be stored covered in the refrigerator for 1–2 days.

Toss all ingredients together and serve.

Fresh Fruit Salsa

(UNDER 30 MINUTES)
MAKES ABOUT 2½ CUPS

½ cup finely diced pineapple

1 clove garlic, pressed through garlic press

½ cup finely chopped mango

½ cup finely chopped papaya (optional)

⅓ cup raspberries

1–2 serrano chiles, minced

½ cup chopped red bell pepper, roasted (see pages 34–36)

⅛ teaspoon ground cardamom

1 teaspoon red wine vinegar

2 tablespoons Key lime juice

¾ cup finely chopped cilantro

Calories per serving (⅓–½ cup): 42
Total fat: 0g
Saturated fat: 0g
Calories from fat: 1
Protein: 1g
Carbohydrates: 11g
Dietary fiber: 1g
Sugars: 8g

The sweetness of the fruit is especially tasty over fish and provides a welcome condiment for taming hot, spicy dishes such as the Chile-Lime Tofu on page 146. To capture the refreshing flavors of fresh, ripe fruit, serve immediately.

Gently toss all ingredients together; serve immediately.

Basic Pesto

(UNDER 30 MINUTES)
MAKES 1¾ CUPS

2 cups basil leaves, firmly packed

4 cloves garlic, pressed through garlic press

1 cup Italian parsley leaves

2 tablespoons grated Parmesan cheese

½ teaspoon salt

½ teaspoon pepper

¼ cup extra-virgin olive oil

¼ cup piñons

Calories per serving (2 tablespoons): 35

Total fat: 3g
Saturated fat: 0g
Calories from fat: 30
Protein: 1g
Carbohydrates: 1g
Dietary fiber: 0g
Sugars: 4g

Pesto sauce not only adds pizazz to fish, chicken, salads, and pasta, but is also beneficial for your health. Garlic, fresh herbs, and piñons all contain powerful antioxidants.

Process all the ingredients in a food processor until they are completely minced and the pesto has the consistency of a thick puree.

Roasted Pepper Cilantro Sauce Supreme

MAKES 4–5 CUPS

1 cup boiling water

10 small sun-dried tomatoes

3 large red bell peppers

5 poblano peppers

1 medium yellow onion

1½ cups fresh cilantro leaves and a few tender stems, loosely packed

½ cup fresh Italian parsley leaves, packed

2 cloves garlic, pressed through garlic press

1 teaspoon lemon zest

½ cup lemon juice

1 teaspoon salt

¼ cup piñons

3 tablespoons extra-virgin olive oil

Calories per serving (⅓–½ cup): 99

Total fat: 7g

Saturated fat: 1g

Calories from fat: 58

Protein: 2g

Carbohydrates: 10g

Dietary fiber: 3g

Sugars: 5g

The deep green hue of the poblanos against bright red bell peppers adds excitement to any entrée. Serve over fish, chicken, or an open-faced sandwich. My son Alex, who has always loved slipping into the kitchen to nab a bite of whatever I was making, discovered that it also makes a great dip for tortilla chips and vegetables. This recipe makes more than enough for serving over 6 portions of chicken, so use the leftovers as a dip or cut the recipe down by about one third.

Pour the boiling water over the sun-dried tomatoes; allow 10 minutes for hydrating. Drain and set aside.

Roast bell peppers, poblanos, and onion according to the directions on pages 34–37. The red bell peppers and onions will not be processed but will be mixed into the sauce. Coarsely chop the red bell peppers, finely chop the onion, and set aside.

In the work bowl of a food processor, process the rehydrated sun-dried tomatoes, poblanos, cilantro, parsley, garlic, lemon zest, lemon juice, salt, and piñons until the consistency is that of a coarse puree. While adding a steady stream of oil, process until oil is thoroughly mixed in. Scrape into a small bowl and mix in the chopped red bell pepper and onion pieces.

Sunset Sauce

MAKES 5 CUPS

6 large yellow tomatoes, or substitute red tomatoes

2 large red tomatoes

6 large red bell peppers

2 large yellow bell peppers

3 Anaheim or New Mexico green chiles

2 large poblano chiles

1 teaspoon Mexican oregano (rub between fingertips to release flavor)

1 tablespoon epazote leaves, or replace with another teaspoon Mexican oregano (rub between fingertips to release flavor)

½ teaspoon ground cumin

1 tablespoon extra-virgin olive oil

1 large onion, chopped

6 cloves garlic, pressed through garlic press

1 cup minced cilantro leaves, packed

2 tablespoons Key lime juice

Zest from 1 Key lime

Salt and pepper

Calories per serving
(⅓–½ cup): 91
Total fat: 2g
Saturated fat: 0g
Calories from fat: 20
Protein: 4g
Carbohydrates: 18g
Dietary fiber: 5g
Sugars: 8g

Inspired by our Arizona sunsets, this beautifully colored sauce with mellow, well-balanced flavors complements fish, chicken, or vegetables. To enhance the flavors of the tomatoes and peppers, I roast them whole on a grill or under the broiler. Dried epazote leaves lend a distinct flavor. They can be difficult to find; try your local Mexican market. If you can't find epazote, don't worry—the sauce is delightful without it, too.

Roast the yellow and red tomatoes, red and yellow bell peppers, green chiles, and poblanos according to the directions on pages 34–36. Cut 3 of the red and 1 of the yellow roasted bell peppers into strips, or coarsely chop, and reserve for later use. (They will not be processed in food processor.)

Place the roasted tomatoes, remaining bell peppers, green chiles, Mexican oregano, epazote, and cumin in the bowl of a food processor; pulse a few times to coarsely puree.

In a large saucepan, sauté onion and garlic in olive oil over medium heat for about 2 minutes, or until the onions are crisp, yet tender. Add the puree and sauté over medium-low heat for about 5 minutes to heat and blend the flavors. The onions should remain somewhat crunchy.

Remove from burner and add the reserved bell peppers, cilantro, lime juice, zest, salt, and pepper. Serve ½ cup over salmon, chicken, or vegetables, or use as a dip. Store remainder in refrigerator for up to 2 days, or freeze for up to 6 months.

Chipotle-Lime Rub

MAKES APPROXIMATELY ⅓ CUP

2 tablespoons Key lime zest

2–3 dried chipotle
chile peppers

¾ teaspoon whole
cumin seeds

½ teaspoon whole
coriander seeds

1½ teaspoons oregano leaves

12 black peppercorns

1 teaspoon onion flakes

2 sun-dried tomatoes
(not the moist variety)

½ teaspoon mustard powder

2 teaspoons sugar

1 teaspoon garlic powder

2 teaspoons salt

There is no other chile like the wonderfully fragrant chipotle, with its distinctive woody flavor to warm your emotions and wake up your senses. It is a smoked, dried, red jalapeño, but oh how the drying and smoking change its character. This rub can be used not only on chicken, fish, and meats, but also in sauces, marinades, and salad dressings. A little goes a long way. Since I use it extensively, I usually triple this recipe whenever I make it. Be cautious while working with the chiles. You may choose to wear gloves, but don't touch your eyes or lips! Make sure to wash your hands thoroughly after working with chiles.

Dry the lime zest according to the directions on page 39. Toast the chipotles, cumin, coriander, and oregano, according to the directions on pages 38–39, to release their flavors.

Place zest, chipotles, cumin, coriander, oregano, peppercorns, onion flakes, and sun-dried tomatoes in a coffee or spice grinder (see page 14). Grind until the consistency resembles that of a fine powder. Transfer the mix to a cup or small bowl. Add the mustard powder, sugar, garlic powder, and salt, and thoroughly mix. Store the rub in an airtight container in the refrigerator or freezer. It will keep for up to a month.

5

CHAPTER

Soups and Salads

Black Bean Soup

SERVES 8

1 dried ancho chile pepper

2 cups dry black beans

10 cups water

1 onion, quartered

4 cloves garlic, bruised
(press with the flat side of a knife
until juice is released)

1 teaspoon dried epazote
(rub between fingertips
to release flavor),
or 3 teaspoons fresh (optional)

1½ teaspoons Mexican
oregano (rub between
fingertips to release flavor)

1 teaspoon ground cumin

1 teaspoon thyme (rub between
fingertips to release flavor)

2 bay leaves, broken in half

3 celery ribs with leaves,
cut in halves or thirds

2 teaspoons extra-virgin
olive oil

1 cup minced onion

6 cloves garlic, pressed
through garlic press

2 cups nonfat organic
chicken broth

1 can (15 ounces) diced
tomatoes, or 2 cups
chopped fresh tomatoes

¼ cup dry white wine

Black bean soup and corn tortillas have long been favorites in the Southwest. In developing our soup, I was inspired by the flavorful black bean soup we enjoyed in Oaxaca, Mexico. It was made with pork—and all the saturated fat that goes along with it. To eliminate the saturated fat but achieve that rich flavor, chicken broth is used in this hearty version.

This soup can be very spicy. To cut down on the heat, use just one dried ancho chile and choose the Anaheim green chile over the New Mexico green chile. Epazote may be hard to find; check in your local Mexican market. It adds a distinct flavor, but the soup is also very tasty without it. See pages 34–38 for instructions for roasting the green chiles, red bell pepper, and yellow squash. Add a couple dollops of yogurt to each individual serving, to aid in digesting the beans and cut down on gas. Serve this soup with corn tortillas and Easy Day Salad (see page 85).

To bring out the flavor of the ancho chile, toast it before using in the soup. See toasting instructions on page 38. It is not necessary, but it does enhance the flavor.

Sort through beans; remove rocks, twigs, shriveled beans, etc. In a colander, rinse the beans with cold water. Transfer beans to a large pot and add 10 cups of water. Add the ancho chile pepper, onion, bruised garlic, epazote, oregano, cumin, thyme, bay leaves, and celery. Bring to a boil. Turn heat to low and simmer for 2–3 hours, or until beans are soft and tender.

In a small saucepan over medium heat, add olive oil and immediately stir in minced onion and pressed garlic. Sauté until onions are a little limp. Add the sauté, chicken broth, tomatoes, and wine

3 Anaheim or New Mexico green chiles, roasted, peeled, seeded, and chopped, or 1 can (4 ounces) chopped green chiles

½ cup cilantro leaves

¼ cup Key lime juice

Salt

Freshly ground black pepper

GARNISH

⅓ cup crumbled goat feta cheese, or ¾ cup plain goat yogurt

1 large red bell pepper, fresh or roasted, sliced

1 yellow squash, roasted and coarsely chopped

¼ cup chopped cilantro

¼ cup chopped green onions (include some green)

1 Hass avocado, chopped

4 Key limes, quartered

Calories per serving: 234
Total fat: 6g
Saturated fat: 2g
Calories from fat: 50
Protein: 12g
Carbohydrates: 37g
Dietary fiber: 10g
Sugars: 6g

to the beans and cook over low heat for about 5 minutes. Remove from heat and cool for about 30 minutes. Remove bay leaves and ancho chile. Remove the stem—and, if desired, the seeds—from the chile.

To achieve a creamy soup with a little bit of texture, blend about ¾ of the bean mixture (reserving the rest of the whole beans to give the soup some textural interest). In a blender, place the ancho and green chiles, cilantro, lime juice, and 2 cups of the soup mixture. Since the beans may be hot, place the lid on the blender container and loosen the center cap a bit to allow the steam to escape and not pop off the lid. Take care to avoid being burned. Blend until smooth, then pour back into the soup pot. Repeat this process with the remainder of the soup mixture until you achieve the consistency you like. Add salt and pepper.

Serve in individual bowls and attractively garnish with goat feta cheese or a swirl of plain goat yogurt, and accent with a few red bell pepper slices, squash, cilantro, green onions, and avocados. Pass the lime pieces to squeeze juice over the avocado.

Chicken Barley Soup

SERVES 6

8 cups defatted chicken broth
or fat-free packaged broth

½ cup unhulled barley

2 celery ribs, coarsely sliced

2 carrots, coarsely sliced

1 large onion, coarsely sliced

1 cup chopped tomatoes

5 leaves kale, cut into
1-inch strips, or 1 bag
(6 ounces) spinach

2 cups poached chicken

1 pound firm organic tofu,
drained and broken up, or
1 can of pinto beans, drained

1 crookneck squash, sliced

½ cup minced basil
or cilantro leaves

1 Hass avocado,
sliced and chopped

2–3 Key limes, halved

Calories per serving: 323
Total fat: 11g
Saturated fat: 2g
Calories from fat: 96
Protein: 27g
Carbohydrates: 33g
Dietary fiber: 8g
Sugars: 6g

It may be tempting to throw everything in the soup pot at once, but then the barley and vegetables would soak up the fat, and most of the healthy substances would be cooked out of the vegetables. Instead, poach a chicken the day before making chicken soup, so the broth can be defatted and included in the recipe. This doesn't take any more work, just planning. The vegetables have more texture in this soup than in traditional chicken soup. Years ago, my friend Dolores Rivas Bahti taught me a technique that preserves nutrients in cooked vegetables. Instead of adding quick-cooking vegetables to soup, place them in individual bowls and pour the soup over the vegetables. That's what is suggested in this recipe. The squash will be firmer and the spinach will still have some life. See Poached Chicken and Chicken Broth, page 138, for the defatted chicken broth and poached chicken needed for this recipe.

In a heavy soup pot, pour in the chicken broth, then add barley and celery to the broth. Bring to a boil, turn the heat to low, and simmer for 30 minutes. Add carrots and simmer for another 5 minutes. Add onion, tomatoes, kale (if you replace this with spinach, don't add it now), chicken, and tofu or pinto beans. Simmer on low for 5 minutes. Remove from heat.

Place squash and spinach (if using spinach) in individual soup bowls. Ladle hot soup over the vegetables and sprinkle with basil or cilantro. Top with avocados and squeeze lime juice over avocados.

Spicy Yam Soup

SERVES 8

3 large garnet yams

3 cups organic nonfat milk

1 cup organic firm tofu, drained

3 tablespoons organic nonfat, non-instant dry milk

1 jalapeño pepper, diced

Extra-virgin olive oil, sprayed from oil pump

1 large onion, diced

6 cloves garlic, pressed through garlic press

1 teaspoon thyme

1 cup diced celery

1 cup (or more) water or nonfat organic chicken broth

2 tablespoons sherry

2 cups cauliflower florets, broken into bite-size pieces

10 Swiss chard leaves, torn into inch-wide strips

1 cup organic soy milk

1 teaspoon ground pepper

½ cup basil leaves, torn into tiny pieces

1 teaspoon umeboshi pickled plum paste

2 tablespoons organic tamari soy sauce (low-sodium)

This bountiful, rich-tasting soup could stand on its own as a main entrée. Enjoyably tart and salty, pickled plum paste is a necessary ingredient that transforms the taste of tofu into a yogurt- or sour cream-like flavor. It is a traditional Japanese food used not only for flavoring but also as a tonic and is believed to rid the body of toxins. Look for it in the Asian food section of grocery stores.

Preheat oven to 350 degrees F. With a sharp knife, prick the yams in several places so they will bake evenly and won't explode. Bake on a cookie sheet for about 40 minutes or until soft. Remove the yams, peel, and cut into quarters.

In the work bowl of a food processor, process yams with 1 cup milk, the tofu, dry milk, and jalapeño pepper until creamy-smooth; set aside.

Lightly spray a heavy soup pot with olive oil; sauté the onion, garlic, thyme, and celery over medium heat for 3–4 minutes. Add water or broth, sherry, and cauliflower; bring to boil. Turn heat to low. Add chard leaves and cook until the chard is slightly limp.

GARNISH

½ cup chopped
fresh tomatoes

½ cup minced poblano peppers,
or Anaheim or New Mexico green
chiles, roasted (see roasting
instructions, pages 34-36)

1 large red bell pepper,
sliced and cut in half

½ cup thinly sliced
green onions

¼ cup chopped cilantro

Calories per serving: 135
Total fat: 2g
Saturated fat: 0g
Calories from fat: 19
Protein: 10g
Carbohydrates: 21g
Dietary fiber: 3g
Sugars: 5g

When the chard is cooked, use a spatula to scrape the yam puree from the food processor into the soup pot, along with the remainder of the milk, the soy milk, and ground pepper; stir until well blended. Stirring frequently, heat until the soup is piping hot.

Remove from burner and mix in basil, pickled plum paste, and soy sauce. Pickled plum paste is salty, so taste before adding the soy sauce. Serve in individual soup bowls and accent with garnishes.

Chilled Spicy Cantaloupe Soup

(UNDER 30 MINUTES)
SERVES 4

½ cup organic soft silken tofu, or regular soft tofu packed in water

½ cup nonfat plain yogurt

¼ teaspoon umeboshi pickled plum paste

1–2 cubes crystallized ginger

1 tablespoon frozen apple juice concentrate, for sweetness (optional)

2 fresh oranges, seeds and skins removed

1 medium cantaloupe, peeled, seeded, and cut into chunks

GARNISH

2 cups raspberries or blueberries

¼ cup mint leaves

Calories per serving: 169
Total fat: 2g
Saturated fat: 2g
Calories from fat: 14
Protein: 6g
Carbohydrates: 36g
Dietary fiber: 8g
Sugars: 28g

For a refreshing change, enjoy this visually appealing and delicious cold soup. It could also pass as a dessert.

If using tofu that comes in a tub of water, pat with a paper towel to remove some of the water. In a blender, blend the tofu, yogurt, plum paste, and ginger until ginger is completely blended.

Add the apple juice concentrate, oranges, and cantaloupe, and blend until mixture is smooth. If the blender container is not large enough, process in a couple of batches. Transfer the blended mixture into a large bowl; cover and chill in the refrigerator for 1–2 hours.

If the soup has separated during refrigeration, stir vigorously to blend. Ladle into individual bowls, add berries, and garnish with fresh mint leaves. Serve immediately.

The apple juice will add 6 calories, 1g carbohydrate, and 1g sugar per serving.

Corn Chowder

SERVES 8

1 red bell pepper

3 green chiles, or 1 can (4 ounces) green chiles

8 ounces extra-firm organic tofu, drained

1½ cups low-sodium, nonfat organic chicken broth

2 teaspoons umeboshi pickled plum paste

3 cups corn kernels

2 teaspoons New Mexico red chile powder

1 teaspoon Mexican oregano

½ teaspoon ground cumin

1½ tablespoons olive oil

¾ cup chopped yellow onion

½ cup chopped celery

1 large red potato, finely chopped

2 cups chopped Roma tomatoes

3 tablespoons macadamia nut butter

Freshly ground black pepper

Sea salt

½ cup chopped cilantro or basil leaves, for garnish

Calories per serving: 388
Total fat: 14g
Saturated fat: 2g
Calories from fat: 119
Protein: 13g
Dietary fiber: 8g
Sugars: 3g
Carbohydrates: 57g

Traditional corn chowders are made with butter, whole milk, and cream. This chowder replaces those ingredients with soy milk, olive oil, and macadamia nut butter, which fit into an anti-inflammatory diet due to having less saturated fat, a much higher content of monounsaturated fat, and a favorable ratio of Omega-6/Omega-3 EFAs. Macadamia nut butter gives that creamy coating butter supplies that is difficult to match. You can use either Anaheims or New Mexico green chiles, either fresh or frozen corn, and either mild, medium, or hot chile powder.

Roast the red bell peppers and green chiles (if using fresh chiles, not canned) according to directions on pages 34–36; coarsely chop and set aside. In a blender, blend the tofu, 1 cup chicken broth, pickled plum paste, 1½ cups of the corn, chile powder, oregano, and cumin until smooth.

In a large saucepan, over medium heat, sauté the onion and celery in olive oil until soft. Add the reminder of the chicken broth and corn, along with the potato and tomatoes, and simmer over medium heat for about 5 minutes.

Pour the tofu mixture into the saucepan, and cook until the corn is done, stirring frequently, for approximately 5 minutes. Stir in macadamia butter and mix thoroughly. Mix in the roasted peppers and freshly ground black pepper. If necessary, add a pinch of sea salt.

Remove from burner and serve with a sprinkling of cilantro or basil.

Black Bean Pasta Salad with Tangy Cilantro Sauce

SERVES 6

TANGY CILANTRO SAUCE

1 cup boiling water

10 sun-dried tomatoes

1½ cups packed fresh cilantro

4 large fresh garlic cloves, cut in thirds

1 teaspoon ground cumin

1 teaspoon Mexican oregano

⅓ cup piñons

⅓ cup red wine vinegar

⅓ cup lemon juice

1 teaspoon salt

2 tablespoons extra-virgin olive oil

SALAD

3 Anaheim or New Mexico green chiles, or 1 can (4 ounces) chopped green chiles

1 poblano chile

1 large red bell pepper

4 ounces whole-grain quinoa pasta or sprouted-wheat pasta (penne or rotini)

1 teaspoon olive oil

1 can (15 ounces) black beans, drained and rinsed

1 cup fresh or frozen corn, cooked and drained

¾ cup chopped celery

½ cup chopped red onion

1 can (4½ ounces) sliced olives

2 large tomatoes, chopped

For lunch or dinner, this Southwest salad is a winner. To achieve a full-bodied Southwest flavor, roast the peppers. To reduce fat, eliminate the piñons from the sauce.

To prepare the Tangy Cilantro Sauce, pour boiling water over sun-dried tomatoes; soak for 10 minutes to rehydrate. With a slotted spoon, remove the rehydrated tomatoes from the tomato broth; set aside. Save the broth.

In a food processor bowl, place cilantro, garlic, cumin, oregano, piñons, vinegar, lemon juice, salt, and rehydrated sun-dried tomatoes. Add the olive oil in a steady stream while processing until the mixture is a rough puree. Allow the flavors to develop for about an hour in the refrigerator.

If you are using fresh green chiles instead of canned, roast them now according to the directions on pages 34–36. The poblano chile and red bell pepper may be used raw or roasted for this salad; if you prefer roasted peppers, roast them now. Next, chop the green chiles, poblano, and red bell pepper. To prepare the salad, cook the pasta to al dente by following package directions, then drain and place in a serving bowl. Add 1 teaspoon or more of olive oil and toss.

½ cup finely sliced green onions

Pinch of sea salt

Freshly ground pepper

1 Hass avocado, sliced, peeled, and chopped

Calories per serving: 470
Total fat: 18g
Saturated fat: 2g
Calories from fat: 153
Protein: 14g
Carbohydrates: 69g
Dietary fiber: 15g
Sugars: 7g

Drain and rinse the beans in a colander, then add to pasta. Mix in ⅔ of the Tangy Cilantro Sauce and the remaining ingredients except for the avocado; toss. Upon tasting, add more lemon juice or Tangy Cilantro Sauce if desired.

Refrigerate, covered, for at least 1 hour for the flavors to meld together. Just before serving, mix in the avocado. Serve cold or at room temperature.

Black Bean Salad

2 cups cooked black beans, drained and rinsed

2 medium cloves garlic, pressed through garlic press

½ cup chopped roasted green chiles, fresh or canned (see pages 34–36)

½ cup chopped red bell pepper

½ cup chopped poblano pepper

¼ cup thinly sliced green onions

1½ cups chopped tomatoes

½ teaspoon ground cumin

1 teaspoon dried Mexican oregano leaves

½ cup chopped cilantro

1 ear roasted sweet corn, cut from the cob (see pages 34–36), or ¾ cup frozen corn, cooked and drained

1 teaspoon New Mexico red chile powder, or Chipotle-Lime Rub (see page 70)

¼ cup Key lime juice

1 tablespoon extra-virgin olive oi (or more, to taste)l

Pinch of sea salt

Freshly ground black pepper

1 Hass avocado

Calories per serving: 245
Total fat: 8g
Saturated fat: 1g
Calories from fat: 143
Protein: 9g
Carbohydrates: 37g
Dietary fiber: 10g
Sugars: 3g

Black beans create the canvas for a splattering of brightly colored vegetables. You will not only appreciate the aesthetics, but will enjoy the combinations of flavors and the health-promoting benefits from hundreds of nature's natural medicines—phytochemicals, including many antioxidants—which work in synergy to reduce the risk of heart disease, cancer, and other chronic diseases. Although this takes less than 30 minutes to prepare, it should sit for an hour before serving. The New Mexico red chile powder can be either mild, medium, or hot.

Toss all ingredients together except for the avocado and chill for 1 hour. Just before serving, slice, peel, and chop the avocado, then add it to the salad and gently toss.

Leone's Fiesta Coleslaw

(UNDER 30 MINUTES)
SERVES 4

3 cups shredded green cabbage

¼ cup sliced red onion

1 medium-size carrot, shredded

1 medium tart apple (Pippin, Granny Smith, or Jonathan), finely chopped

½ cup thinly sliced red bell pepper

½ cup peeled, julienne-cut jicama

2–3 tablespoons cider vinegar, or to taste

2–3 tablespoons water

1 teaspoon sugar

Pinch of sea salt

Freshly ground black pepper

Calories per serving: 59
Total fat: 0g
Saturated fat: 0g
Calories from fat: 0
Protein: 2g
Carbohydrates: 14g
Dietary fiber: 4g
Sugars: 2g

Growing up, I don't believe a day went by that we didn't eat cabbage. Our family had a garden and a fruit orchard from which we canned and froze fruits and vegetables for the year. Since there was an abundance of cabbage in our family's garden when I was growing up in Edwardsville, Illinois, Mom and I would make sauerkraut in large stoneware crocks, and it would be available throughout the year. She prepared sautéed cabbage and, almost daily, coleslaw. Cabbage is a vegetable high in nutrients that you, too, should try to include in your diet on a regular basis. It's not only one of the healthiest foods, but it is readily available and inexpensive. I hope you enjoy my mom's coleslaw recipe with a Southwest twist.

You need to follow your taste buds in determining how much vinegar and water to add. So, taste as you go. Mix all ingredients and serve at room temperature or chilled.

Easy Day Salad

(UNDER 30 MINUTES)
SERVES 4

SALAD

⅓ cup chopped onions

2 tablespoons lemon juice

1 bag Earthbound Farm or Trader Joe's organic herb salad

1 large tomato, chopped

½ Hass avocado, peeled, sliced, and chopped

½ cup chopped cucumber

2 tablespoons crumbled goat feta cheese

Sprinkling of flaxmeal (optional)

DRESSING

2–3 tablespoons extra-virgin olive oil

3–4 tablespoons lemon juice, or 1 tablespoon cider vinegar

Pinch of sea salt

Freshly ground pepper

Calories per serving: 134
Total fat: 11g
Saturated: 2g
Calories from fat: 108
Protein: 2g
Carbohydrates: 8g
Dietary fiber: 3g
Sugars: 2g

I prepare this salad almost every day. Simple and refreshing, it goes with any entrée. If I have leftover steamed peas or asparagus, I add that. A sprinkling of flaxmeal is a tasty addition and adds Omega-3 EFAs.

Soak the chopped onion in the 2 tablespoons of lemon juice for 5 minutes. Place the soaked onion and all other salad ingredients in a large salad bowl. Pour olive oil and lemon juice or vinegar over the salad; add salt and pepper. Toss and serve.

Spinach Fruit Salad

(UNDER 30 MINUTES)
SERVES 6

DRESSING

¼ cup orange juice

1 teaspoon orange zest

¼ cup Key lime juice

2 tablespoons extra-virgin olive oil

1 medium garlic clove, bruised (press with the flat side of a knife until juice is released)

1 teaspoon mustard powder

Salt and freshly ground black pepper

SALAD

1 papaya, peeled

1 bag (6 ounces) baby spinach

¼ cup diced red onion

1½ cups sliced organic white peach, with skin

1 cup fresh blueberries

¼ cup dried cranberries, or chopped dates

¼ cup toasted or raw piñons (see toasting instructions, page 39)

¼ cup crumbled goat feta cheese

Calories per serving: 216
Total fat: 12g
Saturated fat: 3g
Calories from fat: 106
Protein: 4g
Carbohydrates: 26g
Dietary fiber: 7g
Sugars: 16g

With a balance of sweetness and citrus tartness, this colorful salad makes a perfect accompaniment for fish. Take advantage of the abundance of fresh summer fruits by pairing this dish with the Pistachio-Crusted Salmon on page 114. It is also the perfect salad to top with cooked salmon that has been chilled. Use leftovers or prepare the Margarita Salmon with Fresh Fruit Salsa on page 119, substituting this salad for the salsa. The sweet fruit and the salmon make a tasty combination.

Whisk together all of the dressing ingredients and allow flavors to meld for a couple of hours at room temperature. Store any leftover dressing in the refrigerator after use.

Wash the outside of the papaya with a vegetable wash and dry with a paper towel. Cut it in half, scoop out the seeds and stringy fiber, slice, peel, and cut into bite-size pieces. Place papaya pieces and all other salad ingredients in a large bowl, add dressing, and gently toss.

6

CHAPTER

Chile Rellenos and Quesadillas

Piñon-Crusted Chile Rellenos

SERVES 5

FILLING

½ cup whole-grain quinoa (not flakes)

1 cup nonfat organic chicken broth

1 tablespoon extra-virgin olive oil

½ teaspoon New Mexico red chile powder (mild, medium, or hot)

½ teaspoon ground cumin

½ teaspoon Mexican oregano leaves (rub between fingertips to release flavor)

½ teaspoon thyme leaves (rub between fingertips to release flavor)

½ cup minced cilantro leaves

4 large basil leaves, minced

¼ teaspoon salt

¼ teaspoon freshly ground black pepper

Zest from 1 Key lime

½ cup chopped roasted onion

1 cup roasted and chopped Roma tomatoes

4–6 cloves garlic, roasted and chopped

½ cup chopped roasted red bell pepper

1 small zucchini squash, roasted and chopped

¼ cup piñons, toasted

(continued)

Wrapped in a crust of toasted corn tortillas, these rellenos are bursting with appetizing flavors. The vegetables are roasted to maintain firmness, while bringing out the sweetness of the onion and mellowing the garlic to a nutty flavor. Buttery piñons, a good source of Omega-3 EFAs, are toasted to develop their flavor and add crunch to the stuffing, while gluten-free quinoa, a full protein with a pleasing flavor, keeps it all in harmony. As an alternative, consider adding leftover salmon, chicken, or black beans to the stuffing. For easier stuffing, choose straight (not crinkly) peppers. Note that the onion, tomatoes, garlic, bell pepper, zucchini, and poblano peppers will need to be roasted before you begin this recipe, and the piñons will need to be toasted. For roasting the vegetables and toasting the piñons, see roasting instructions, pages 34–38, and toasting instructions, page 39. Rub the oregano and thyme between your fingertips to release their flavors. Add a quick Easy Day Salad to round out this meal (see page 85).

Preheat oven to 375 degrees F. To prepare the filling, stir together the quinoa, chicken broth, olive oil, chile powder, cumin, oregano, and thyme in a heavy 1½-quart saucepan. Turn the heat to high and bring to a boil. Reduce heat to simmer. Cover with a lid and simmer, stirring occasionally, for about 15 minutes, or until the liquid is almost all absorbed by the quinoa. Remove from burner, toss with a fork, and let sit a few minutes. The grain will soak up the remainder of the water. Transfer the quinoa to a medium-size mixing bowl, add all other filling ingredients except the toasted piñons, and toss together.

Toast the corn tortillas by placing them directly on the racks of the oven. Toast until they are slightly crispy on the outside but still a little pliable. They will become more brittle when cooled.

COATING

5 corn tortillas

½ cup grated
Parmesan cheese

⅓ cup cilantro leaves

⅛ teaspoon salt

1 teaspoon Mexican oregano

¼ teaspoon ground cumin

½ teaspoon thyme

¼ cup piñons, toasted

FOR ASSEMBLY

1 teaspoon butter

5 large poblano
peppers, roasted

¾ cup whole-grain
yellow cornmeal

1 egg

2 tablespoons extra-virgin
olive oil

¼ cup Key lime juice

½ teaspoon salt

½ teaspoon New Mexico
red chile power (mild,
medium, or hot)

1 teaspoon Mexican oregano

¼ teaspoon freshly ground black
pepper

1 tablespoon extra-virgin
olive oil

Calories per serving: 604
Total fat: 34g
Saturated fat: 6g
Calories from fat: 295
Protein: 17g
Carbohydrates: 68g
Dietary fiber: 10g
Sugars: 9g

Break tortillas into small pieces, producing 1 cup of broken pieces.

In a food processor, process the tortilla pieces, Parmesan cheese, cilantro, salt, oregano, cumin, thyme, and ¼ cup of the piñons to a crumb texture. It will be a bit moist. Transfer the tortilla crumb coating to a small plate and set aside.

Coat the bottom of a 12 x 7½ x 2-inch baking dish with butter. Carefully cut an opening in each poblano, from the stem to within 1 inch of the tip.

Place the cornmeal on a small plate. Whisk together the egg, 2 tablespoons of olive oil, lime juice, salt, chile powder, oregano, and pepper. Pour this mixture into a small shallow bowl.

Add the remaining ¼ cup of piñons to the filling and mix thoroughly. Stuff the peppers, causing the openings to gap. Roll each poblano side to side in the cornmeal while avoiding the gap with the filling, then dip in the egg mixture—again, cover just the chile, not the filling. Allow the egg mixture to drip off, then roll the pepper side to side in the tortilla crumb coating. Place in the buttered pan, open side up.

After all poblanos are in the pan, add remaining filling to overstuff the peppers. Some may spill over into the pan, and that's okay. Follow with a drizzle of olive oil. Place on center rack of the oven and bake for 10 minutes. This will be enough time to make the crust a bit crispy and the stuffing just warm enough to eat. Transfer to individual plates or serve on a tray.

Bobby's Spinach Quesadillas with Black Bean Piping

(UNDER 30 MINUTES)
SERVES 2

4 sun-dried tomatoes

1 cup water

⅓ cup grated Soy-Sation lite mozzarella or pepper Jack soy cheese, or replace with an equal amount of grated firm goat cheese, or mix together half soy and half goat cheese

2 whole wheat or sprouted-grain tortillas (9-inch size)

2 cups fresh baby spinach leaves, or chopped spinach leaves

⅓ cup thinly sliced red or yellow onion

⅓ cup thinly sliced red bell pepper

¼ cup bottled salsa or Fresh Salsa

Calories per serving: 269
Total fat: 7g
Saturated fat: 0g
Calories from fat: 69
Protein: 15g
Carbohydrates: 37g
Dietary fiber: 4g
Sugars: 3g

When, Bobby, my son-in-law, is on his way to Tucson, he will call ahead and request quesadillas. He confesses that until he married Elicia, he was a fast-food junkie and that he never equated what he was eating with how he was feeling. His diet frequently included deep-fried chimichangas, fried fish tacos, Big Macs and French fries, processed packaged foods, chips, dips, and whatever else was quick—and very few fruits and vegetables. When he was hungry, he didn't really care what he ate to satisfy his hunger. Under his new diet of about seven years, he relates feeling better and having more energy. He told me, "I don't feel as well or have as much energy when I eat fast food as I do when eating healthy. Also, what Elicia prepares tastes a whole lot better than what I was accustomed to eating." I hope you, too, will enjoy the taste and health benefits derived from slightly cooked, tender baby spinach in these quick and easy-to-prepare quesadillas. Spinach is one of the powerhouse vegetables. It is extremely low in calories and packed full of nutri- ents. Add a touch of flavor and a festive accent to quesadillas or to the rims of serving plates by adding a zigzag pattern of Black Bean Piping (recipe follows). Look for healthy bottled salsa containing no vegetable oils or make your own Fresh Salsa (page 65). A side of black beans and a salad provides a well-rounded meal and will keep you from eating too many quesadillas!

Rehydrate the sun-dried tomatoes by soaking them for about 10 minutes in 1 cup of water that has been brought to boiling. When they are rehydrated, drain thoroughly and chop; set aside. If using half soy cheese and half goat cheese, mix together and set aside.

Leaving a 1-inch border, sprinkle half of each tortilla with cheese, which acts as a barrier that prevents the tortilla from becoming soggy from the filling. On that same half, add a couple of layers of spinach (it will cook down) followed by layers of the rehydrated tomatoes, onion, and bell pepper, then sprinkle the remaining soy cheese on top of the vegetables.

Heat a 12-inch heavy skillet or griddle over medium heat; do not add oil. Heat the quesadilla until the tortilla becomes warm and pliable. Fold the empty half of the tortilla over the filling and press down with a wide spatula. With the spatula, flip the quesadilla and press down again. Continue warming and turning the quesadilla until the outside is lightly toasted and the cheese is melted. If the heat is too high, you will burn the tortilla before the filling is cooked.

Remove the quesadilla from the skillet and allow it to cool for 5 minutes. Cut into quarters and serve with salsa.

Black Bean Piping
MAKES 1⅓ CUPS

1 can (15 ounces) black beans, drained (reserve broth)

½ teaspoon salt

½–1 teaspoon New Mexico red chile powder (mild, medium, or hot)

¼ teaspoon garlic powder

1 teaspoon ketchup

Calories per serving: 13
Total fat: 0g
Saturated: 0g
Calories from fat: 0
Protein: <1g
Carbohydrates: 5g
Dietary Fiber: <1g
Sugars: <1g

Add all ingredients to blender container and blend until the mixture becomes a thick and smooth puree, adding 1 tablespoon or more of the reserved broth to achieve the correct thickness. Taste and adjust seasonings. Place in a squeeze bottle used for food decorating and pipe away. This will keep for a couple of days if you clean out the bottle cap or transfer the mixture to a covered bowl.

Variation—Salmon Quesadilla

(UNDER 30 MINUTES)
SERVES 2

Calories per serving: 490
Total fat: 19g
Saturated fat: 2g
Calories from fat: 179
Protein: 43g
Carbohydrates: 46g
Dietary fiber: 5g
Sugars: 4g

Salmon is a flavorful complement to spinach and will add Omega-3 EFAs and protein. Prepare the Spinach Quesadilla (page 91) and add 4 ounces of flaked, leftover salmon (one option is to prepare the salmon according to Salmon with Sunset Sauce on page 123, but eliminate the sauce). After cooking, add a couple of slices of avocado and a squeeze of lime juice to this quesadilla as a garnish for a wonderfully satisfying and healthy entrée.

Variation—Broccoli Quesadilla

(UNDER 30 MINUTES)
SERVES 2

Calories per serving: 270
Total fat: 7g
Saturated fat: 0g
Calories from fat: 66
Protein: 16g
Carbohydrates: 37g
Dietary fiber: 4g
Sugars: 3g

Broccoli is a super food and has been hailed as the best plant food of all. It is an excellent source of fiber. It also delivers plentiful amounts of vitamins A and C and folate (folic acid). Follow the same instructions as for the Spinach Quesadilla on page 91, but substitute 1 cup of finely chopped, uncooked broccoli florets for the spinach.

Variation—Squash Quesadilla

(UNDER 30 MINUTES)
SERVES 2

Calories per serving: 270
Total fat: 7g
Saturated fat: 0g
Calories from fat: 66
Protein: 16g
Carbohydrates: 37g
Dietary fiber: 4g
Sugars: 3g

Summer squash is a good source of folic acid (folate), vitamin C, and beta-carotene (vitamin A, which reduces inflammation, boosts the immune system, and protects against cancer and other diseases). You will enjoy the health benefits from these colorful quesadillas along with the wonderfully satisfying flavors. Follow the same instructions as for the Spinach Quesadilla on page 91, but substitute ½ cup of thinly sliced raw zucchini and ½ cup of thinly sliced raw crookneck squash for the spinach.

Portobello Mushroom Quesadilla

SERVES 8

3 portobello mushrooms, 4–5
inches in diameter

1 medium eggplant, unpeeled

½ red bell pepper

1 medium red onion

16 sun-dried tomatoes

1 cup boiling water

½ cup grated Soy-Sation
premium mozzarella soy cheese

1 cup grated Soy-Sation lite
pepper Jack soy cheese

6 whole wheat tortillas
(9-inch size)

1 cup bottled salsa or Fresh
Salsa (page 65)

Calories per serving: 230
Total fat: 6g
Saturated fat: 0g
Calories from fat: 68
Protein: 12g
Carbohydrates: 31g
Dietary fiber: 5g
Sugars: 4g

These quesadillas take a bit more time because the mushrooms and vegetables are roasted beforehand. To save time, roast them the day before and store covered in the refrigerator. Once the ingredients are ready, it takes only minutes to create a quesadilla. You may replace one of the soy cheeses with firm goat cheese.

Roast the mushrooms, eggplant, bell pepper, and onion (see roasting instructions, pages 34–37); the eggplant should not be peeled. Chop the bell pepper after roasting and separate the onion into rings. Re-hydrate the sun-dried tomatoes by soaking them for about 10 minutes in the cup of water that has been brought to a boil. Drain, thoroughly chop, and set aside. Mix the cheeses together and set aside.

Leaving a 1-inch border, sprinkle half of each tortilla with cheese, which acts as a barrier that prevents the tortilla from becoming soggy from the filling. On that same half, add layers of mushrooms, eggplant, bell pepper, onion, and tomato, then sprinkle the remaining soy cheese on top of the vegetables.

Heat a 12-inch heavy skillet or griddle over medium heat; do not add oil. Heat the quesadilla until the tortilla becomes warm and pliable. Fold the empty half of the tortilla over the filling and press down with a wide spatula. With the spatula, flip the quesadilla and press down again. Continue warming and turning the quesadilla until the outside is lightly toasted and the cheese is melted. If the heat is too high, you will burn or toast the tortilla before the filling is cooked.

Remove the quesadilla from the skillet and allow it to cool for 5 minutes. Cut the quesadillas into fourths and serve with salsa.

Cold Tuna Salad Chile Rellenos

1 can (12 ounces) organic albacore solid white tuna in olive oil or water, drained

2 heaping tablespoons grapeseed oil Vegenaise

2 tablespoons extra-virgin olive oil

1 large red bell pepper

¾ cup finely chopped red cabbage

2 medium celery ribs, minced

½ cup minced cilantro leaves

6–8 basil leaves, finely torn

4 green onions, finely chopped

¾ cup finely chopped crookneck squash

¼ cup dried cranberries or raisins (optional)

2 tablespoons Key lime juice

1 cup chopped Hass avocado

4 cups baby greens or herb salad mix

4 large poblano chiles, roasted, peeled, and seeds removed (see pages 34–36)

Salt and pepper

2 teaspoons finely chopped pistachios or piñons

2 small peaches, sliced

1–2 cups raspberries

Calories per serving: 445
Total fat: 22g
Saturated fat: 3g
Calories from fat: 230
Protein: 28g
Carbohydrates: 28g
Dietary fiber: 11g
Sugars: 14g

SERVES 4

These colorful chile rellenos are refreshing and crisp, perfect for serving on a hot summer day. Add a side of mixed peaches and raspberries for a wonderful complement of flavors and colors. Cabbage goes well with fish and is full of antioxidants. There is some evidence that red cabbage may aid in the prevention of Alzheimer's disease. The American Institute for Cancer Research bills it as a top food in the prevention of certain cancers, and tuna is rich in Omega-3 EFAs. The grapeseed oil Vegenaise is a mayonnaise substitute, available at natural foods markets. What more can you ask for than great taste, beautiful color, and a load of health-promoting ingredients? This dish may be prepared a few hours ahead of time and refrigerated. Be sure to include some of the green when you chop the green onions.

In a medium-size bowl, break up the tuna pieces and thoroughly mix with the Vegenaise and olive oil. Finely chop the red bell pepper. Mix the bell pepper, cabbage, celery, cilantro, basil, onions, squash, and dried cranberries or raisins, if you are using them, into the Vegenaise mixture. In a separate bowl, pour lime juice over the avocado pieces and carefully toss to coat. Allow the avocado to absorb the lime juice for a few minutes, then add this to the tuna salad and gently toss to mix.

On each individual salad plate, place a small bed of salad greens. Carefully cut an opening from the stem to within 1 inch of the tip of each poblano. Position the poblano atop the greens, then overstuff it with the tuna salad, being careful not to rip the poblano. I always tuck the sides of the chile into the stuffing to keep the sides from flopping open. Sprinkle each chile relleno with salt, pepper, and ½ teaspoon of pistachios or piñons. Arrange the sliced peaches next to the relleno and scatter raspberries over the peaches.

Enchiladas, Tacos, and More

Roasted Red Bell Pepper Chipotle Enchilada Sauce

MAKES APPROXIMATELY 5 CUPS

1 large red bell pepper

4–5 medium Roma tomatoes

½ cup chopped Vidalia or other sweet onion

6 medium cloves garlic, pressed through garlic press

2 teaspoons extra-virgin olive oil

2 tablespoons ketchup

1 teaspoon Mexican oregano (rub between fingertips to release flavor)

1 teaspoon ground cumin

1⅔ cups Santa Cruz Chipotle Chili Paste

2 cups nonfat organic chicken broth

1 tablespoon Key lime juice

Salt and freshly ground black pepper

Calories per serving: 63
Total fat: 1g
Saturated fat: 0g
Calories from fat: 13
Protein: 2g
Carbohydrates: 13g
Dietary fiber: 3g
Sugars: 6g

Enchiladas are easy to make and are always a welcome meal for friends and family, or great for a party dish. Leftover chicken, fish, beans, and vegetables make quick enchiladas and become a new dish. Chipotle-flavored dishes are a favorite among our family, and homemade enchilada sauce is a real treat! Use it in any enchilada recipe or serve over chicken, fish, or meat. This also makes a tasty addition to chicken soup. Santa Cruz Chipotle Chili Paste is used for ease of preparation. The best tasting enchiladas are made with homemade enchilada sauce, but Rosarita and Hatch canned enchilada sauces make good substitutes, and their ingredients are fairly healthy.

Roast red bell pepper and tomatoes according to directions on pages 34–36. After roasting, chop the tomatoes and set the bell peppers and tomatoes aside.

In a medium-size saucepan, over medium-high heat, sauté the onion and garlic in oil until crisp, yet tender. Add the roasted tomatoes, ketchup, oregano, cumin, chipotle paste, and chicken broth and stir. Simmer for 30 minutes. Transfer to a blender.

Add the prepared red bell pepper and the lime juice to the mixture in the blender; blend until smooth. Stir in salt and pepper. Use sauce immediately or store in refrigerator for up to 2 days or freeze in 1-cup portions for up to 8 months.

Flat Enchiladas

SERVES 8

1 medium eggplant

1 red bell pepper

2 small zucchini

1 small yellow squash

½ cup thinly sliced green onions (include some green)

2 teaspoons extra-virgin olive oil

8 corn tortillas

2 teaspoons extra-virgin olive oil

2–4 cups shredded chicken

4–5 cups homemade enchilada sauce (see Roasted Red Bell Pepper Chipotle Enchilada Sauce, page 99), or canned Rosarita or Hatch enchilada sauce

4 large basil leaves, finely torn, one per enchilada

Unbleached parchment paper

GARNISH

½ cup cilantro leaves

½ Hass avocado, sliced and chopped

1–2 tablespoons finely chopped red onion

¼ cup goat feta cheese

Calories per serving: 262
Total fat: 8g
Saturated fat: 2g
Calories from fat: 66
Protein: 17g
Carbohydrates: 37g
Dietary fiber: 9g
Sugars: 11g

These enchiladas are overstuffed, and a single one will be enough for two people. There's nothing like a warm, flavorful corn tortilla. However, they are high in starch and have a glycemic load of about 10 for each tortilla. Carbohydrates are good for you, but carbohydrates with high glycemic loads should be eaten in combination with foods containing soluble fiber. By combining soluble fiber (available in vegetables) with starchy foods (corn tortillas), the glucose entering the bloodstream is slowed down. Thus, less insulin is produced.

Roast the eggplant, bell pepper, zucchini, and yellow squash according to the directions on pages 34–38. After roasting, transfer to a medium-sized bowl, add the green onions, and then toss the vegetables in 2 teaspoons of olive oil.

Preheat oven to 350 degrees F. Oil the tortillas with 2 more teaspoons of olive oil and place in the oven on a cookie sheet. Bake until the tortillas are pliable, about 3 minutes. Remove from the oven, stack on a plate, and set aside.

In a medium-size bowl, toss the shredded chicken with ½ cup of the enchilada sauce. Pour the remaining sauce into another bowl.

Dredge one tortilla through the remaining enchilada sauce and place on 2 large oven-safe platters or a jellyroll pan. Cover the tortilla with the mixed vegetables, then spread chicken over the vegetables and cover the chicken with more vegetables. Sprinkle with torn basil leaves.

Dredge another tortilla through the enchilada sauce and place on top of the vegetables. Follow the same procedure to make 3 more enchiladas.

Pour the remaining enchilada sauce equally over the enchiladas; cover with an appropriately sized piece of parchment paper and heat in the oven until warm, 5–10 minutes. Remove from oven and top with garnishes. Cut each in half and serve.

Salmon with Asparagus Enchiladas

(UNDER 30 MINUTES)
SERVES 4

1½ pounds cooked, flaked salmon (see Salmon with Sunset Sauce, page 123, but eliminate sauce)

1 teaspoon extra-virgin olive oil

24 asparagus spears

1 tablespoon extra-virgin olive oil

Salt

3½–4 cups Roasted Red Bell Pepper Chipotle Enchilada Sauce (see page 99), or canned Rosarita or Hatch enchilada sauce

8 corn tortillas

1 tablespoon extra-virgin olive oil

½ cup grated goat cheese

2 cups chopped crookneck squash

¼ cup finely chopped red bell pepper

1 clove garlic, pressed through garlic press

1 teaspoon Key lime juice

1 teaspoon extra-virgin olive oil

¼ cup finely sliced green onions, include a little green

¼ cup finely chopped cilantro or basil leaves

Leftover salmon or chicken makes great-tasting enchiladas and saves time. In addition to these enchiladas, I have come up with a number of variations, which follow this recipe. It is easy to make a couple of different kinds of enchiladas at the same time, and the potpourri of flavors adds to the enjoyment. Salmon enchiladas are a good source of protein, vitamin K, vitamin B12, phosphorus, selenium, vitamin A, vitamin C, beta carotene, and folate.

In traditional enchiladas, corn tortillas are fried for flavor and to make them pliable for rolling. In my enchilada recipes, the tortillas are heated in the oven with a slight amount of oil. Heating brings out the flavor of the corn and allows the tortilla to be rolled. The corn tortillas account for 130 of the calories and 25 grams of the carbohydrates. If you eat only one enchilada and add ½ cup of black beans on the side, you will cut the calories by 200 and carbohydrates by 8 grams, and you will still have 14 grams of fiber. Add a tossed green salad with olive oil and lemon juice for the perfect combination.

Preheat oven to 350 degrees F. Prepare the salmon (as directed in the Salmon with Sunset Sauce recipe, but without the sauce), or if you have leftover salmon from another meal, use those leftovers.

Coat a heat-safe serving platter that will accommodate 8 rolled enchiladas with 1 teaspoon of olive oil.

**1 Hass avocado,
sliced and chopped**

1 Key lime

Calories per serving: 677
Total fat: 30g
Saturated fat: 7g
Calories from fat: 260
Protein: 45g
Carbohydrates: 66g
Dietary fiber: 16g
Sugars: 20g

Rinse the asparagus with water and trim by snapping off the ends (not the tips). This procedure will naturally eliminate any tough ends. If you want a clean cut, trim after you snap. Lay the asparagus on a broiler pan or cookie sheet, brush lightly with 1 tablespoon of olive oil, and sprinkle sparingly with salt. Roast in the oven until crisp yet tender, about 8 minutes.

In a saucepan over medium heat, warm the enchilada sauce. Brush both sides of the tortillas lightly with 1 tablespoon of olive oil and heat in the oven on a cookie sheet until the tortillas are pliable for rolling, about 3 minutes. Remove from the oven and stack them on a plate.

Dip one of the prepared tortillas through the enchilada sauce and place it in the baking pan. Place 3 asparagus stalks in the middle of the tortilla and line about 3 ounces of salmon down the middle. Roll the tortilla and place it seam-down on the pan. Repeat this procedure with the remaining tortillas. Pour the remaining enchilada sauce over the filled tortillas and top with a sprinkling of goat cheese.

Mix the squash, red bell pepper, garlic, lime juice, and 1 teaspoon of olive oil in a small bowl. Attractively arrange this mixture around the enchiladas in the pan. Cover and bake until the cheese melts and the salmon is warm, about 10 minutes.

Remove from the oven and dress with chopped onions, cilantro or basil leaves, and avocado. Squeeze fresh Key lime juice over the garnish and serve immediately.

Calories per serving: 667
Total fat: 30g
Saturated fat: 7g
Calories from fat: 260
Protein: 44g
Carbohydrates: 64g
Dietary fiber: 15g
Sugars: 18g

Variation—Spinach Enchiladas

(UNDER 30 MINUTES)
SERVES 4

Use the same ingredients as in the Salmon with Asparagus Enchiladas, substituting a handful of fresh spinach for the asparagus in each enchilada. The spinach will wilt slightly from the heat.

Calories per serving: 664
Total fat: 30g
Saturated fat: 7g
Calories from fat: 260
Protein: 44g
Carbohydrates: 63g
Dietary fiber: 15g
Sugars: 18g

Variation—Basil Enchiladas

(UNDER 30 MINUTES)
SERVES 4

Use the same ingredients as in the Salmon with Asparagus Enchiladas, substituting 4–5 fresh basil leaves for the asparagus in each enchilada.

Calories per serving: 688
Total fat: 30g
Saturated fat: 7g
Calories from fat: 264
Protein: 44g
Carbohydrates: 69g
Dietary fiber: 18g
Sugars: 21g

Variation—Eggplant Enchiladas

SERVES 4

Use the same ingredients as in the Salmon with Asparagus Enchiladas, substituting 3–4 slices of roasted eggplant for the asparagus in each enchilada (see roasting instructions, pages 34–36).

Chicken and Spinach Enchilada Casserole

SERVES 8

CREAM SAUCE

1 pound organic extra-firm tofu

1 tablespoon umeboshi pickled plum paste

1½ teaspoons Mexican oregano leaves (rub between fingertips to release flavor)

½ teaspoon sage (rub between fingertips to release flavor)

½ teaspoon rosemary (rub between fingertips to release flavor)

½ teaspoon thyme (rub between fingertips to release flavor)

½ teaspoon marjoram (rub between fingertips to release flavor)

¼ teaspoon nutmeg

½ teaspoon ground cumin

6–8 medium cloves garlic, peeled and cut into thirds

1 cup nonfat organic chicken broth

¾ cup minced cilantro leaves

1 cup finely chopped onion

1¼ cups grated soy cheese

2 cups organic boneless, skinless, poached chicken breast, or leftover chicken

3 Anaheim or New Mexico green chiles, roasted and finely chopped, or 3 canned green chiles

(continued)

Soy shares the stage with animal protein in these mildly spicy enchiladas. As a result, some animal fat has been replaced with the health-promoting fats contained in soy. Soy, tomatoes, and red bell peppers are among the most beneficial plant foods in building a strong defense against cancer and cardiovascular disease.

Soy-Sation premium mozzarella or pepper Jack soy cheese make good alternatives to regular cheese, adding creaminess and flavor to the cream sauce. If using the Roasted Red Bell Pepper Chipotle Enchilada Sauce, prepare it ahead of time. To make the poached chicken, see Poached Chicken and Chicken Broth on page 138; see pages 34–36 for directions on roasting the green chiles. This dish freezes nicely and tastes great reheated. Add a side of black beans and a tossed green salad dressed with olive oil and lemon to boost the protein by 10 grams and the fiber by 8 grams.

Preheat oven to 350 degrees F.

To make the cream sauce, drain water from the tofu and pat with a paper towel. In a blender, blend the drained tofu, plum paste, oregano, sage, rosemary, thyme, marjoram, nutmeg, cumin, garlic, and chicken broth until smooth and creamy. Pour the sauce into a medium mixing bowl. Stir in the cilantro, onion, and soy cheese. Remove 1 cup of the sauce and set aside for the top layer of the casserole.

Shred the poached chicken by holding a piece of chicken and pulling the meat away with a fork. Gently fold the chicken and green chiles into the bowl of cream sauce: set aside.

Coat the bottom and sides of a 13 x 9 x 2½-inch baking dish with olive oil.

FILLING

1 teaspoon extra-virgin olive oil

4 cups Roasted Red Bell Pepper Chipotle Enchilada Sauce (see page 99), or use canned Rosarita or Hatch enchilada sauce

12 corn tortillas, torn into pieces

1 bag (6 ounces) fresh baby spinach, or 2 packages (10-ounce size) frozen spinach, thawed, with water squeezed out

1 can (14½ ounces) diced tomatoes, drained

GARNISH

1 large tomato, chopped

½ cup thinly sliced green onions (include some green)

1 red bell pepper, thinly sliced

¼ cup minced cilantro leaves

1 can (4 ounces) black olives, sliced

1 cup small crookneck squash, thinly sliced

1 Hass avocado, peeled, sliced, then chopped

2 Key limes

Calories per serving: 461
Total fat: 21g
Saturated fat: 3g
Calories from fat: 180
Protein: 26g
Carbohydrates: 47g
Dietary fiber: 8g
Sugars: 11g

Set aside ⅓ cup of enchilada sauce for the top of the casserole. Cover the bottom of the pan with ½ cup of enchilada sauce. Lay a blanket of tortilla pieces over the sauce and press them into the sauce. Pour ½ cup of enchilada sauce over the tortilla pieces. Spread half of the bowl of the cream mixture over the sauce. Add a layer of spinach. If using fresh spinach, press leaves into the sauce. The bulk of the fresh spinach will fill up the casserole but will cook down. Evenly spread half of the drained tomatoes over the spinach and top with another ½ cup of enchilada sauce.

Starting with tortilla pieces, create a second layer using the same procedure as in the first layer. To top off the casserole, press a layer of tortilla pieces into the enchilada sauce, follow with the reserved cup of cream sauce, and accent with a drizzle of the reserved enchilada sauce.

Cover the pan with a lid or aluminum foil and bake for 40 minutes, or until the edges are bubbly and the center is hot. While the casserole cooks, toss together all of the garnish ingredients except for the squash, avocado, and lime; set aside.

Remove the casserole from the oven and remove the pan lid or aluminum foil—caution: hot steam, don't get burned! Spread the squash on top of the casserole and re-cover with foil, leaving the casserole out of the oven. The squash slices will cook slightly. In about 5 minutes, sprinkle the garnish mixture over the casserole. Place avocados on top and squeeze lime juice over the avocados. Serve immediately.

Dominic's Portobello Mushroom Enchilada Casserole

SERVES 8

3–4 portobello mushrooms,
4–5 inches in diameter

Extra-virgin olive oil

Salt

Pepper

CREAM SAUCE

1 pound organic extra-firm tofu

1 cup nonfat organic chicken
broth or vegetable broth

4 cloves garlic, cut into thirds

2 teaspoons
umeboshi plum paste

½ teaspoon ground cumin

1 teaspoon Mexican
oregano (rub between
fingertips to release flavor)

12 Swiss chard leaves

1 tablespoon extra-virgin
olive oil

4 cloves garlic, pressed
through a garlic press

1 large onion, finely chopped

½ cup grated Soy-Sation
premium mozzarella soy cheese

½ cup grated Soy-Sation lite
pepper Jack soy cheese

(continued)

These enchiladas were created especially for my friend Dominic Wallen, a vegetarian who loves portobello mushrooms. He rated this as the best recipe in the book. It freezes nicely, and leftovers taste great!

Portobello mushrooms contain protein and are an excellent source of zinc and potassium. Add ½ cup of black beans and a tossed green salad dressed with olive oil and lemon to boost the protein by 10 grams and fiber by 8 grams. Umeboshi pickled plum paste is an essential ingredient in the cream sauce. It transforms the taste of tofu into a yogurt- or sour cream-like flavor, and is found in the Asian food section of most grocery stores. If you like, you can substitute ½ cup of grated Monterey Jack for one of the soy cheeses.

Preheat the broiler to high heat. Gently wash mushrooms with cold water. Trim ½ inch from the tip of each stem. Cut into ½-inch slices and lightly brush with olive oil. Sprinkle lightly with salt and pepper.

Arrange the mushroom slices on the broiler pan, not touching each other. Position the broiler pan on the top oven rack and broil for about 2 minutes, or until the mushrooms are sizzling and turning a bit golden. Turn and repeat on other side. They should be tender, yet firm. Cut the roasted mushrooms into bite-size pieces. Reserve ½ cup for the garnish and set the remainder aside.

Turn off the broiler and preheat oven to 350 degrees F.

To make the cream sauce, drain the water from the tofu and pat with a paper towel. In a blender, blend the tofu, chicken or vegetable broth, 4 cut-up cloves of garlic, plum paste, cumin, and

FILLING

Extra-virgin olive oil

3½ cups Roasted Red Bell Pepper Chipotle Enchilada Sauce (see page 99), or use canned Rosarita or Hatch enchilada sauce

12 corn tortillas, torn into pieces

1 can (14½ ounces) diced, fire-roasted tomatoes, drained

1 large red bell pepper, chopped

GARNISH

⅓ cup finely sliced green onions (include some green)

1 cup chopped red bell pepper, raw or roasted (see roasting instructions, pages 34–36)

¼ cup minced cilantro leaves

1 Hass avocado, peeled, sliced, and chopped

1 Key lime

Calories per serving: 322
Total fat: 13g
Saturated fat: 2g
Calories from fat: 106
Protein: 16g
Carbohydrates: 43g
Dietary fiber: 9g
Sugars: 9g

oregano until smooth. Pour into a medium-sized bowl; set aside. Clean the chard by removing the stems and any tough veins, then cut the leaves into 1-inch strips. In a 5-quart saucepan, heat the tablespoon of olive oil over medium heat and sauté the pressed garlic and onion for 3 minutes. Add the chard and sauté until slightly limp. Remove from the burner and scrape the tofu mixture into the sauté. Add the cheeses and thoroughly mix.

Coat a 13 x 9 x 2½-inch glass baking dish with olive oil. Set aside ⅓ cup of the enchilada sauce for the top of the casserole. Pour half of the remaining enchilada sauce in the bottom of the pan. Next, make a single layer of tortilla pieces over the sauce; press the tortillas into the sauce. Spread ⅓ of the creamy mixture over the tortillas. Cover the creamy mixture with half of the tomatoes. Sprinkle with half of the red bell pepper, follow with half of the unreserved chopped mushrooms, and then pour the other half of the enchilada sauce over the layer. Repeat the layers of the creamy mixture, tomatoes, bell pepper, and mushrooms.

For the top layer (third layer), place a layer of tortilla pieces. Pour the remaining creamy mixture over the top. Spread the reserved enchilada sauce over the top, making sure the tortillas are completely covered with sauce. Cover and bake casserole at 350 degrees F for 40 to 45 minutes, or until heated through and bubbly. While the casserole cooks, toss together all of the garnish ingredients with the exception of the avocado and lime; set aside.

After the casserole is ready, remove from the oven and allow it to cool for 5 minutes. Sprinkle with garnish mixture, including the reserved mushrooms. Top off with avocados and squeeze lime juice over the avocados. Serve immediately.

Leftover Salmon Tacos

(UNDER 30 MINUTES)
SERVES 4

4 corn tortillas

8–12 ounces leftover
cooked salmon (see Salmon
with Sunset Sauce, page 123,
but eliminate the sauce)

1½ cups thinly
shredded cabbage

⅓ cup thinly sliced onions,
soaked in 1 teaspoon Key lime
juice for a few minutes

½ red bell pepper, thinly sliced

4 slices of Hass avocado
(½ inch wide)

½ cup bottled salsa or Fresh
Salsa (page 65)

Calories per serving: 233
Total fat: 10g
Saturated fat: 2g
Calories from fat: 92
Protein: 16g
Carbohydrates: 18g
Dietary fiber: 4g
Sugars: 2g

These are simple and delicious. The tortilla is heated, but the stuffing is enjoyed cold. To save time, place the ingredients in serving bowls. Heat the tortillas and cover them with a clean napkin or towel to keep warm. Have each person fix his or her own taco. For a deliciously satisfying complement to fish tacos, add a side of Leone's Fiesta Coleslaw (page 84).

Follow the heating and folding instructions for the tortillas on page 40. When the tortilla is warm, fill it with the salmon, cabbage, onion, red bell pepper, and avocado. Dress with salsa. Fold and serve.

Leftover Fish or Chicken Tacos

(UNDER 30 MINUTES)
SERVES 4

4 corn tortillas

2 cups salmon or chicken chunks

12 basil leaves, torn into small pieces, or ½ cup chopped cilantro leaves

⅓ cup thinly sliced onions, soaked in 1 teaspoon Key lime juice for a few minutes

1 red bell pepper, roasted and sliced (see roasting instructions, pages 34–36)

4 slices Hass avocado (½ inch thick)

¼ cup goat feta cheese

Bottled salsa or Fresh Salsa (page 65)

Calories per serving: 224
Total fat: 10g
Saturated fat: 2g
Calories from fat: 91
Protein: 18
Carbohydrates: 15g
Dietary fiber: 3g
Sugars: 1g

Roasted red bell peppers and basil are a delicious combination and a refreshing complement to fish or chicken. If you have leftovers from a chicken or salmon recipe, use them. If you don't have leftovers, prepare Salmon with Sunset Sauce (see page 123) or Chicken with Roasted Pepper Cilantro Sauce Supreme (see page 133), eliminating the sauce for whichever recipe you choose.

Follow the heating and folding instructions for the tortillas on page 40. Fill the warm tortillas with the salmon or chicken, basil, onion, bell pepper, avocado, and cheese. Dress with salsa. Fold and serve.

To save time, place the ingredients in serving bowls. Heat the tortillas and cover them with a clean napkin or towel to keep warm. Have each person fix his or her own taco.

Black Bean Tostadas

(UNDER 30 MINUTES)
SERVES 3

3 corn tortillas

1 can (15 ounces) black beans, or replace with Quick No-Refried Black Beans (see page 167)

1 small garlic clove, pressed through garlic press, or ½ teaspoon garlic powder

½ teaspoon Mexican oregano (rub between fingertips to release flavor)

1/4 teaspoon ground cumin

1/3 cup bottled salsa or Fresh Salsa (page 65)

½ green chile, canned or freshly roasted, then chopped (see roasting instructions, pages 34–36)

¼ cup chopped cilantro leaves

¼ cup thinly sliced onions, soaked in 1 teaspoon Key lime juice for a few minutes

1 cup fresh lettuce

¼ cup sliced radishes

⅓ cup chopped tomatoes

3 slices Hass avocado (½ inch thick)

Calories per serving: 288
Total fat: 4g
Saturated fat: 1g
Calories from fat: 32
Protein: 15g
Carbohydrates: 51g
Dietary fiber: 16g
Sugars: 1g

Our family eats black beans with corn or hemp tortillas, but they are also tasty wrapped in sprouted-grain flour tortillas.

Preheat oven to 350 degrees F. Toast the tortillas in the oven, directly on the oven rack, until they are crisp like chips.

If using canned beans, drain and save the juice. In a small bowl, mash the beans with a fork or vegetable masher. Place the beans in a small saucepan with the garlic, oregano, and cumin. Heat the bean mixture over medium-low heat until warm; add enough of the reserved bean juice (or a little water) to achieve a creamy consistency and to prevent the beans from burning. Stir in a small amount of salsa.

Remove from the burner and spread beans on top of each toasted tortilla. Top with the green chile, cilantro, onion, lettuce, radishes, tomato, and avocado, and add the remaining salsa. Serve warm.

Leftover Chicken or Tofu Wraps

(UNDER 30 MINUTES)
SERVES 2

2 whole-grain or sprouted-grain
flour tortillas (9-inch size)

4 Hass avocado slices
(½ inch thick)

6 ounces leftover chicken
(shredded), or organic
baked, pressed, and
seasoned tofu (cubed)

6 thin red bell pepper slices

1 cup fresh spinach
or baby greens

½ cup chopped tomatoes

6 thin onion slices, soaked
in 1 teaspoon Key lime juice
for a few minutes

½ cup bottled salsa or Fresh
Salsa (page 65)

Calories per serving: 407
Total fat: 11g
Saturated fat: 2g
Calories from fat: 96
Protein: 39g
Carbohydrates: 37g
Dietary fiber: 4g
Sugars: 3g

Wraps are nothing more than filled and rolled flour tortillas. Here's a very healthy version. The nutritional analysis is based on a 9-inch tortilla, which accounts for a large portion of the carbohydrates. If you don't have leftover chicken, prepare Chicken with Roasted Pepper Cilantro Sauce Supreme (see page 133), but eliminate the sauce. You could prepare the Chile-Lime Tofu (see page 146) to create seasoned tofu. Stuff these wraps with a generous amount of vegetables and you can even share half a wrap with a friend.

Follow the warming and rolling instructions for the tortillas on page 40. Mash the avocado pieces and spread over the tortillas. Fill with chicken or tofu, red bell pepper, spinach or greens, tomatoes, and onion, and roll it up. Serve with salsa for dipping.

Fish

Pistachio-Crusted Salmon

SERVES 6

1 tablespoon butter

6 Alaskan red sockeye salmon fillets (4 ounces each), without skins

¼ cup Key lime juice

4 corn tortillas

1 clove garlic, pressed through garlic press

½ cup grated Asiago cheese

½ cup unsalted raw pistachios, toasted (see page 39)

⅓ cup cilantro leaves

Zest from 1 Key lime

⅛ teaspoon salt

⅔ cup whole-grain yellow cornmeal

¼ teaspoon salt

¼ teaspoon fresh ground black pepper

1 egg

2 tablespoons extra-virgin olive oil

2 teaspoons New Mexico red chile powder (mild, medium, or hot)

1 teaspoon Mexican oregano (rub between the palms of hands to release flavor)

3 tablespoons extra-virgin olive oil

A crusted mélange of pistachios, corn tortillas, and Asiago cheese offers a slight crunch and imparts a complementary flavor to the succulent taste of salmon. This is considered a special occasion dish. It is high in calories due to the fat and carbohydrates, but it contains anti-inflammatory nutrients, including monounsaturated fats. Both salmon and pistachios provide Omega-3 EFAs. The mix of sweet fruit flavors with a splash of citrusy undertones makes the Spinach Fruit Salad (see page 86) a perfect match for the salmon. Round off with a few roasted zucchini and roasted red bell pepper slices.

Preheat oven to 350 degrees F. Use enough of the 1 teaspoon of butter to coat the bottom an 8 x 14 x 2-inch baking pan.

Place the salmon fillets on a nonreactive platter. Pour 2 tablespoons of lime juice over the fillets and set aside.

Slightly toast the corn tortillas on a cookie sheet in the oven at 350 degrees F for 5 minutes. They need to be crisp on the outside but still pliable beneath the crust—not crispy like a corn tortilla chip.

Place the tortillas, garlic, cheese, pistachios, cilantro, lime zest, and ⅛ teaspoon of salt in a food processor work bowl and process to a crumb mixture. Transfer to a 10-inch plate.

On another 10-inch plate, mix together the cornmeal, ¼ teaspoon of salt, and freshly ground pepper.

In a small mixing bowl, beat the egg with a fork or wire whisk. Whisk in the 2 tablespoons of olive oil, chile powder, oregano, and the remaining lime juice. Transfer to a shallow 8-inch bowl.

Calories per serving: 498
Total fat: 28g
Saturated fat: 6g
Calories from fat: 248
Protein: 39g
Carbohydrates: 23g
Dietary fiber: 4g
Sugars: 2g

Dust the fish with cornmeal mixture. Dip the fillets in the egg mixture, allowing excess mixture to drip off. Coat with the pistachio mixture, making sure the fillets are fully covered. Place in the prepared baking dish with space between the fillets. Drizzle 3 tablespoons of olive oil over the fillets. Bake uncovered for about 10–15 minutes. Remove from the oven and allow to sit for 5 minutes before serving. Once the fillets are removed from the oven, they will continue to cook; you don't want to overcook salmon.

Sable Fish with Summer Squash

(UNDER 30 MINUTES)
SERVES 2

Unbleached parchment paper

1⅓ cup thinly sliced crookneck squash

1⅓ tablespoons finely chopped poblano pepper (seeds and veins removed)

2 tablespoons finely chopped Vidalia or other sweet onion

1 clove garlic, pressed through garlic press

¼ cup chopped Roma tomato

2 sable fish (black cod) fillets (4 ounces each), with skins

2½ teaspoons Key lime juice

Zest from 1 Key lime

2 teaspoons chopped chives

2 teaspoons dill

Salt and freshly ground pepper

10 papaya slices

2 teaspoons minced cilantro leaves

2 slices Hass avocado, chopped

This dish offers such a beautiful presentation with hues of greens, orange, yellow, and red—whew, lots of different colors, an indication of an array of phytochemicals! Sable fish is also known as butter fish, and for good reason. It is buttery-rich and boasts one of the highest amounts of Omega-3 EFAs among fish. A little goes a long way. This dish takes only about 30 minutes prep and baking time, with little cleanup. Parchment is available in a number of widths— 13-inch or 15-inch parchment works fine for this recipe.

Preheat oven to 350 degrees F. Cut an 18-inch length of parchment for each fillet. Fold the rectangle in half, so you will have a folded piece 13 (or 15) x 9. Cut a fat half-heart shape from the folded rectangle, then unfold the heart to prepare the ingredients directly on the parchment. In a medium-size bowl, gently mix together the squash, poblano, onion, garlic, and tomato.

On one side of the heart-shaped paper, place the fish with the skin side down and arrange 1 cup of the vegetable mixture around the fillet. Pour half of the lime juice over the fish and sprinkle with half each of the lime zest, chives, and dill, making sure to get a little on the vegetables. Sprinkle salt over the fish and vegetables followed with freshly ground pepper. Top off fish with half of the papaya slices. Repeat the process for the second fillet.

Calories per serving: 369
Total fat: 26g
Saturated fat: 5g
Calories from fat: 235
Protein: 22g
Carbohydrates: 12g
Dietary fiber: 4g
Sugars: 5g

You will encase the fish and vegetables in the parchment. Fold the empty half of the heart shape back over the prepared fish. Starting at the top of the folded heart at the crease, fold the bottom of the parchment over the top and pinch, making a seam. Continue folding and pinching the edges until you reach the point of the heart. Twist the point of the heart and tuck under. Make sure that the parchment is completely sealed. Place on a cookie sheet on the middle rack of the oven and bake. With the temperature at 350 degrees F, I usually bake 15 minutes per 1-inch thickness of the fish. The parchment will puff up and be somewhat browned. Remove from oven; allow 5 minutes for cooling. Cut open the parchment—be careful not to get burned by the steam. Sprinkle with cilantro and avocado. Serve in parchment on a plate.

Citrus Salmon with Spinach

(UNDER 30 MINUTES)
SERVES 6

Unbleached parchment paper

6 Alaskan red sockeye salmon
fillets (4 ounces each), or
replace with mahi-mahi or halibut

MARINADE

¼ cup fresh grapefruit juice

Salt

Freshly ground black pepper

2–3 medium cloves garlic,
pressed through garlic press

1 teaspoon lemon zest

1 teaspoon Key lime zest

2 teaspoons grapefruit zest

2 teaspoons lemon juice

2 teaspoons Key lime juice

VEGETABLES

6 cups fresh baby spinach
leaves, packed

3 cloves garlic, pressed through
garlic press

⅓ cup thinly sliced red onion

2 tablespoons finely chopped
red bell pepper

2 teaspoons finely chopped
poblano pepper (seeds
and veins removed)

2 teaspoons Key lime juice

Salt and freshly ground pepper

2 teaspoons chives

⅓ cup sliced mango or papaya

¼ cup minced cilantro leaves

½ cup chopped Hass avocado

Grapefruit is the key flavor ingredient in this luscious fish dish. It adds a satisfying citrus flavor that complements the flavor of the salmon. It is a favorite among our friends, and as a plus, contains antioxidants and Omega-3 EFAs. Parchment is available in a number of widths—13-inch or 15-inch parchment works fine for this recipe. It's best if you can allow the fish to marinate for an hour, but if you are in a hurry, let it marinate while you are getting everything else ready.

Preheat oven to 350 degrees F. For each serving, cut a 20-inch piece of parchment. Fold the rectangle in half, so you will have a folded piece 13 (or 15) x 10. Cut a fat half-heart shape from each folded rectangle.

With a chef's tweezers or pliers, remove the bones from the fish. Place the fish in a shallow dish. Pour grapefruit juice over it, tossing the fish in the juice. Arrange the fish pieces in a single layer; sprinkle top side with salt and pepper.

Mix the garlic and the lemon, lime, and grapefruit zests together in a small bowl, then rub onto the top side of the fish. Pour the lemon and lime juices over the fish, being careful not to disturb the zest. Marinate in the refrigerator for 1 hour, if you have time.

On one side of the heart-shape parchment paper, place 1 cup of spinach. Scatter garlic, onion, bell pepper, and poblano pepper over the spinach. Follow with lime juice, salt, and pepper.

Center the fish atop the spinach. Sprinkle with chives; accent with a few slices of mango or papaya.

Calories per serving: 293
Total fat: 15g
Saturated fat: 3g
Calories from fat: 133
Protein: 33g
Carbohydrates: 6g
Dietary fiber: 2g
Sugars: 2g

Fold the empty half of the heart shape over the fish and vegetables to encase them in the parchment. Starting at the top of the folded heart—at the crease—fold the bottom of the parchment over the top and pinch, making a seam. Continue folding and pinching the edges until the point of the heart is reached. Twist the point and tuck under. Make sure that the parchment is completely sealed.

Place on a cookie sheet and set on the middle rack of oven to bake. If the fish is about 1 inch thick, bake for 15 minutes. The parchment will puff up and be somewhat browned. Remove from oven; allow 5 minutes for cooling. Cut open the parchment, being careful not to get burned by the steam, then sprinkle with cilantro and avocado. Serve in parchment on each plate.

Margarita Salmon with Fresh Fruit Salsa

SERVES 6

6 wild Alaskan red sockeye salmon fillets (4 ounces each), with skin

MARINADE

1 tablespoon extra-virgin olive oil

3 cloves garlic, pressed through garlic press

¼ cup tequila

1 teaspoon honey

¼ cup Key lime juice

1 teaspoon Key lime zest

1 tablespoon orange zest

1 tablespoon triple sec (optional)

1 teaspoon New Mexico red chile powder, or 1 tablespoon Chipotle-Lime Rub (see page 70)

½ cup minced cilantro leaves

½ teaspoon Mexican oregano

Salt (omit if using Chipotle-Lime Rub)

1 tablespoon extra-virgin olive oil

White wine

1 Fresh Fruit Salsa recipe (see page 66)

Calories per serving: 312
Total fat: 15g
Saturated fat: 2g
Calories from fat: 132
Protein: 32g
Carbohydrates: 12g
Dietary fiber: 1g
Sugars: 8g

Margarita Salmon is tasty without the Fresh Fruit Salsa, too, but the fruit adds complementary flavors with a touch of sweetness that goes well with fish—not to mention two servings of beneficial fruits and vegetables, essential for a disease-preventive diet. The Chipotle-Lime Rub adds a little heat and that unmistakable smoky chipotle flavor. Or if you use New Mexico red chile powder, you can choose either mild, medium, or hot.

Using a chef's tweezers or pliers, remove the bones from the salmon. Place the salmon in a nonreactive, high-heat-safe casserole dish. Mix together the marinade ingredients in a medium-sized bowl. Pour over the salmon, making sure it is well coated. Cover and marinate for 2 hours in the refrigerator, if you have time; toss occasionally.

Salmon fillets are often uneven. If so, cut off the thinner part of the salmon and cook it for less time. Arrange the salmon skin-side down in the casserole dish and lightly coat the top with oil. If there is not ¼ inch of liquid in the pan, add white wine to make the liquid ¼ inch deep, which will prevent the salmon from sticking.

Preheat broiler to high heat. Place the dish about 4–6 inches under the broiler. Broil 10 minutes per inch of thickness. When cooked, the salmon should be very juicy in the middle or slightly rare.

Serve immediately with ½ cup of Fresh Fruit Salsa spooned over the top of each fillet, or serve the salsa on the side for dipping.

Tangy Tuna Cabbage Salad

(UNDER 30 MINUTES)
SERVES 6

¾ cup sliced red onion

3 tablespoons cider vinegar

1 can (12 ounces) organic albacore solid white tuna in olive oil or water, drained

¾ cup chopped Roma tomatoes

1 cup thinly sliced red bell pepper

3 cups sliced red cabbage

1 cup chopped fresh cilantro leaves, with a few tender stems

2–3 cups halved red seedless grapes

2 tablespoons extra-virgin olive oil

Salt and freshly ground pepper

1 whole Hass avocado

2 tablespoons Key lime juice

2 teaspoons Key lime zest

Calories per serving: 272
Total fat: 14g
Saturated fat: 2g
Calories from fat: 121
Protein: 17g
Carbohydrates: 22g
Dietary fiber: 4g
Sugars: 14g

My husband, who loves cilantro, came up with this tasty one-dish meal. Along with having a gorgeous presentation, it is full of health-promoting substances. The polyphenols in red cabbage act as dietary antioxidants by battling oxidative stress, which causes brain cell damage associated with Alzheimer's disease. There is also evidence that polyphenols protect against cancer, cardiovascular disease, diabetes, and osteoporosis.

Soak the onion slices in the vinegar.

In a large bowl, break up the tuna pieces into a flaky consistency. Add the marinated onion, including the vinegar, and toss. Gently mix in the tomatoes, bell pepper, cabbage, cilantro, and grapes. Pour olive oil over the salad and mix thoroughly, adding salt and pepper to taste. Place salad on individual plates.

Slice, peel, and chop the avocado into bite-size pieces. Top off the salad with chopped avocado and sprinkle with lime juice and zest. Serve immediately, or if you want to chill the salad, hold the avocado and lime until it is served.

Salmon with Sunset Sauce

SERVES 6

6 wild Alaskan red
sockeye salmon fillets (4
ounces each), with skin

½ cup dry white wine

2 cloves garlic, pressed
through garlic press

Salt

Extra-virgin olive oil sprayed
from oil pump

3 cups prepared
brown basmati rice

1 Sunset Sauce recipe
(see page 69)

Calories per serving: 274
Total fat: 6g
Saturated fat: 3g
Calories from fat: 57
Protein: 14g
Carbohydrates: 66g
Dietary fiber: 7g
Sugars: 9g

This is one of the most beautiful culinary presentations in our book, and it doesn't stop with visual appeal. The combination of flavors truly elicits enjoyment for the palate. The Sunset Sauce is full of lycopene, which is heart-healthy and protects against some cancers. Add one of the gala butternut squash recipes (pages 158–160) for a perfect meal.

With a chef's tweezers or pliers, remove bones from the salmon. Place the salmon in a high-heat-resistant glass or other non-reactive casserole dish. Pour wine over the salmon. Use the back of a spoon or your fingers to rub garlic and salt into the flesh of the salmon. Spray or rub the salmon with olive oil.

Preheat broiler to high heat. Place salmon under the broiler and broil for 3–4 minutes, or until it is slightly seared. If necessary, spray olive oil to keep moist.

After searing, remove the salmon from the oven and cover tightly with foil or a casserole lid. Preheat oven to 350 degrees F and bake for 3–5 minutes, depending on thickness of fillets. If unsure, test a piece by cutting into the fillet. Salmon is a very delicate fish and should remain moist or slightly rare in the middle. It will continue to cook slightly out of the oven. Therefore, be careful not to overcook or you will ruin the texture and lose flavor.

Place ½ cup of rice on each plate, top with salmon, and pour ¼–½ cup of Sunset Sauce over the salmon.

Salmon, Broccoli, and Pasta, Olé!

SERVES 4

4 Alaskan red sockeye salmon fillets (4 ounces each), with skins

½–1 cup dry white wine

3 cloves garlic, pressed through garlic press

1 teaspoon New Mexico red chile powder (mild, medium, or hot)

2 cups chopped fresh tomatoes

1 cup finely sliced green onions

Extra-virgin olive oil sprayed from oil pump

2 tablespoons Key lime juice

4 ounces whole-grain pasta (quinoa or sprouted grain)

1 Basic Pesto recipe (see page 67)

2 cups broccoli florets

⅓ cup sliced red bell pepper

Freshly ground black pepper

Sea salt

Calories per serving: 467
Total fat: 23g
Saturated fat: 4g
Calories from fat: 206
Protein: 38g
Carbohydrates: 23g
Dietary fiber: 6g
Sugars: 0g

My friend John Kundrat gave me the idea for this flavorful dish at our daughters' volleyball banquet. It's a tasty combination of healthful ingredients, and the pasta is more of a tasty addition rather than the main ingredient. Cook the pasta and broccoli while the salmon is broiling, to save time.

Preheat broiler to high heat.

Place the salmon skin side down in a 12 x 7½ x 2½-inch glass baking dish. Pour ½ cup of wine over the salmon and rub with garlic. Sprinkle with chile powder and spread tomatoes and onions over the top. Lightly spray the salmon and vegetables with olive oil. If there is not ¼ inch of liquid in the pan, add more wine to make the liquid ¼ inch deep, to prevent the salmon from sticking.

Place the fish about 4–6 inches from the hot broiler and broil for a couple of minutes until onions and tomatoes begin to char. Turn the salmon and vegetables; broil the other side of the fish. Total cooking time should be 10 minutes per inch of thickness of the fish. The fish can be slightly rare in the middle. If not rare, it should definitely be juicy. Once removed from the oven, it will continue to cook slightly. Transfer the fish to a plate and sprinkle with lime juice. When cooled, remove the skin and break the fish into bite-size pieces. Reserve the vegetables and fish broth in the baking dish.

Cook the pasta according to package directions. After draining, transfer to a large nonreactive bowl that will accommodate the salad. Add a little of the prepared pesto sauce, then toss.

In a medium-size pot, insert a vegetable steamer basket. Add water to just below the basket. Add broccoli and bring to a boil over high heat. Reduce heat and steam broccoli for approximately 5 minutes, or until it is bright green and crisp, yet tender. Remove from heat, drain, and transfer to a plate to prevent broccoli from continuing to cook.

Mix the desired amount of pesto sauce with the fish broth, tomatoes, and onions, and add the broccoli and red bell pepper. Toss this in with the pasta. If the sauce needs thinning, add a little dry white wine.

Add the fish to the pasta salad and season with freshly ground pepper. Toss gently to combine. If needed, add more pesto, a pinch or 2 of salt, or additional pepper. Gently toss to combine and serve.

Dr. Smith's Sweet-Hot Salmon

SERVES 8

MARINADE

½ cup honey

1 tablespoon organic tamari soy sauce (low-sodium)

⅛ teaspoon cayenne pepper

2 teaspoons New Mexico red chile powder (mild, medium, or hot)

¼ teaspoon freshly ground pepper

1 teaspoon lemon zest

5–10 drops Tabasco chipotle pepper sauce

1 tablespoon grated ginger

1 teaspoon Worcestershire sauce

8 Alaskan red sockeye salmon fillets (4 ounces each), with or without skins

Dry white wine

4 cups shredded Chinese cabbage

Calories per serving: 321
Total fat: 13g
Saturated fat: 2g
Calories from fat: 115
Protein: 32g
Carbohydrates: 19g
Dietary fiber: 1g
Sugars: 18g

Our good friend Lloyd Smith is not only a great dentist but a fantastic chef. He shared with me his popular salmon dish, and the critics gave it a ten. Serve over shredded Chinese cabbage and add a side of Butternut Squash Couscous (see page 156).

Mix together the marinade ingredients in a medium-size bowl. Set aside.

Remove bones from the salmon with pliers or chef's tweezers. Place the salmon in an appropriate-size casserole dish and coat with the marinade. Refrigerate for 2 hours.

Preheat the broiler to high heat. If there is not ¼ inch of liquid in the casserole dish, add wine to make the liquid ¼ inch deep around the pieces of salmon. Place the dish on the top rack of the oven; the fish should be 4 to 6 inches from the broiler. Broil 10 minutes per inch of thickness of the fish, turning once. When cooked, the salmon should be very juicy in the middle.

Serve over shredded Chinese cabbage.

Rosemary Salmon

(UNDER 30 MINUTES)
SERVES 6

MARINADE

¼ cup packed fresh rosemary leaves

¼ cup extra-virgin olive oil

¼ cup minced basil leaves, or 1 teaspoon dried

4 cloves garlic, pressed through garlic press

1 teaspoon salt

½ teaspoon freshly ground pepper

2 tablespoons lemon juice

1 teaspoon lemon zest

6 Alaskan red sockeye salmon fillets (4 ounces each), with or without skin

White wine as needed

1 lemon, sliced ⅛ inch thick

Calories per serving: 351
Total fat: 22g
Saturated fat: 3g
Calories from fat: 193
Protein: 32g
Carbohydrates: 8g
Dietary fiber: 1g
Sugars: 2g

Before you take the first bite, aromatic rosemary readies your palate for this refreshing entrée. Rosemary, an evergreen, flourishes in our backyard and is available for cooking year-round. Aside from imparting a wonderful scent, it may improve memory and alertness. Even if you don't have time to marinate for the full hour, the salmon will still absorb the rosemary flavor and be delicious.

Preheat oven to 350 degrees F. Heavily bruise the rosemary leaves by crushing them. In a nonreactive bowl, mix the rosemary with other marinade ingredients. Set aside.

With a chef's tweezers or pliers, remove the bones from the salmon. Place the salmon in a glass, refrigerator-to-oven casserole dish. With the back of a spoon or your fingertips, rub the marinade into the flesh of the salmon. Cover and marinate for 1 hour in the refrigerator.

Arrange fish in single layer; don't crowd. If there is not ¼ inch of juice in the pan, add a little white wine to make the liquid ¼ inch deep. Place the casserole dish on the middle rack of the oven. Bake for about 15 minutes basting frequently. Remove from the oven and allow to rest for a few minutes. Accent with lemon cartwheels and serve.

9

Poultry

Cilantro Chicken and Vegetables

SERVES 6

MARINADE

½ cup fresh-squeezed lemon juice

¼ cup extra-virgin olive oil

¾ teaspoon Mexican oregano (rub between fingertips to release flavor)

½ cup minced cilantro leaves, lightly packed

4 cloves garlic, pressed through garlic press

1 teaspoon mustard powder

1 teaspoon salt

Freshly ground black pepper

SKEWERS

1½ pounds organic boneless, skinless chicken breasts

1 red bell pepper, cut into 1½-inch chunks

1 orange bell pepper, cut into 1½-inch chunks

1 poblano pepper, cut into 1½-inch chunks

1 yellow onion, quartered

20 grape or cherry tomatoes

1–2 small crookneck squash, cut into 1-inch pieces

1–2 zucchini squash, cut into 1-inch pieces

If you are a cilantro fan who enjoys its tangy flavor, you will love this recipe. Serve with Southwest Quinoa Pilaf (page 154) and a fresh green salad. Be sure to have bamboo skewers on hand for this recipe.

Combine all of the marinade ingredients in a small nonreactive mixing bowl and set aside.

Rinse chicken breasts under cold water and pat dry with paper towels. Cut the chicken breasts into bite-size pieces and toss in the marinade to coat. Cover and marinate for 2 hours in the refrigerator, tossing frequently. You may also use a Ziploc-type freezer bag to marinate the chicken.

Soak 18 bamboo skewers in water for 15 minutes.

Thread the chicken and the pieces of red and orange bell pepper, poblano, onion, tomatoes, yellow squash, and zucchini onto skewers, making sure you have the same size chicken pieces per skewer to assure even cooking and that all pieces of chicken are separated by pieces of vegetables.

If grilling on a gas or charcoal grill, set at high heat or allow coals to become hot. Put the prepared skewers on the grill and cook until the chicken is browned. Turn and cook the other side for about 2 minutes, or until the chicken is done and moist.

If you broil, preheat the oven to broil at high heat. Place the skewers on the broiler pan as close to the broiler as possible. Allow the chicken to brown slightly. Turn over the chicken pieces and broil until done, 2–3 more minutes.

Calories per serving: 326
Total fat: 14g
Saturated fat: 2g
Calories from fat: 123
Protein: 38g
Carbohydrates: 13g
Dietary fiber: 3g
Sugars: 6g

If using an electric grill, set at high heat and grill until browned on one side, about 4 minutes. Turn and grill on other side until browned, or until the chicken is done but moist.

Serve immediately.

Cilantro Chicken Pasta Salad

SERVES 6

MARINADE

1½ cup lemon juice

¼ cup extra-virgin olive oil

¾ teaspoon Mexican oregano (rub between fingertips to release flavor)

½ cup minced cilantro leaves, lightly packed

4 cloves garlic, pressed through garlic press

1 teaspoon mustard powder

1 teaspoon salt

Freshly ground black pepper

SALAD

1½ pounds organic boneless, skinless chicken breasts

¼ cup minced red onion

¼ cup lemon juice

4 ounces quinoa pasta

2 tablespoons extra-virgin olive oil

1½ tablespoons Key lime juice

2 medium cloves garlic, pressed through garlic press

(continued)

This delicious salad concentrates more on the vegetables, with the pasta to complement the dish. Quinoa is considered a complete protein since it has all eight essential amino acids. Each serving has about 4 ounces of chicken.

In a small nonreactive mixing bowl, combine all of the marinade ingredients and set aside.

Rinse the chicken breasts under cold water and pat dry with paper towels. Cut the chicken breasts into bite-size pieces and toss in the marinade to coat. Cover and marinate for 2 hours in the refrigerator, tossing frequently. You may also use a Ziploc-type freezer bag to marinate the chicken.

To tame a strong onion flavor, soak the red onion in 1 tablespoon of the lemon juice; set aside.

Follow package directions in preparing the pasta with an al dente firmness. Drain and rinse the pasta, transfer to a large bowl, add olive oil, and gently toss. Add Key lime juice, garlic, and the prepared onion, and toss. Allow to sit for about 10 minutes. Toss in the yellow and orange bell pepper, poblano, tomatoes, and the remaining lemon juice. Salt lightly and coarsely grind black pepper generously over the salad. Refrigerate until the chicken is added.

½ **yellow bell pepper,**
coarsely chopped

½ **orange bell pepper,**
coarsely chopped

1 **poblano pepper,**
coarsely chopped

1 **cup chopped tomatoes, or**
grape tomatoes halved

Sea salt

Freshly ground black pepper

5 **large basil leaves, finely torn**

¼ **cup minced cilantro leaves**

Calories per serving: 357
Total fat: 15g
Saturated fat: 3g
Calories from fat: 134
Protein: 39g
Carbohydrates: 16g
Dietary fiber: 4g
Sugars: 2g

When grilling or broiling small chicken pieces, I prefer to thread the pieces onto skewers for easy turning. Prepare 10 bamboo skewers by soaking them in water for 15 minutes. To ensure even cooking, don't pack the chicken pieces too closely together.

If grilling on a gas or charcoal grill, set at high heat or allow coals to become hot. Place the skewers on the grill and cook until the chicken is browned. Turn and cook on the other side for about 2 minutes or until the chicken is done, but still moist.

If you broil, preheat the oven to broil at high heat. Place the skewers on the broiler pan as close to the broiler as possible. Allow the chicken to brown slightly. Turn over the chicken pieces and broil until done, 2–3 minutes.

If using an electric grill, set at high heat and grill until browned on one side, about 4 minutes. Turn and grill on the other side until browned, or the chicken is done but moist.

Take care not to overcook. Overcooked chicken will be rubbery and the flavor will be compromised. The thickness of the pieces will dictate the length of time needed to cook. Also, once removed from the heat, the chicken will continue to cook slightly.

Transfer skewers to a platter to cool. Remove chicken from the skewers and add to the pasta, along with the basil and cilantro. Gently toss until well mixed. To bring flavors together, refrigerate for 1 hour. Serve cold or at room temperature.

Chicken with Roasted Pepper Cilantro Sauce Supreme

SERVES 6

Extra-virgin olive oil

1½ pounds organic boneless, skinless chicken breasts

2 tablespoons lemon juice

2 cloves garlic, pressed though garlic press

½ teaspoon ground cumin

1 teaspoon oregano (rub between fingertips to release flavor)

½ teaspoon sage

½ teaspoon salt

1 teaspoon freshly ground black pepper

¼ cup dry white wine

1 teaspoon extra-virgin olive oil

1 Roasted Pepper Cilantro Sauce Supreme recipe (see page 68)

Calories per serving: 310
Total fat: 13g
Saturated fat: 2g
Calories from fat: 12
Protein: 36g
Carbohydrates: 14g
Dietary fiber: 4g
Sugars: 7g

Golden chicken fillets graced with an autumn-colored sauce will stimulate a mouthwatering sensation, and the flavors will satisfy the most discerning palate. Be generous with this nutrient-dense sauce. It contains an abundance of essential nutrients that work together to promote optimal health. Add the Easy Day Salad on page 85 for a complete meal.

Preheat oven to 350 degrees F. Coat the bottom and sides of an 11 x 7 x 1½-inch casserole dish with olive oil.

Rinse the chicken pieces under cold water and pat dry with paper towels. Cut the chicken into 6 serving pieces, 4 ounces each.

In a small bowl or cup, mix together lemon juice, garlic, cumin, oregano, sage, salt, and pepper. Rub half of the lemon mixture on one side of the chicken breasts. Place the chicken breasts in the casserole dish with the seasoned side down. Pour the wine over the chicken. Rub the teaspoon of olive oil on the chicken breasts and season with the remaining lemon mixture.

Set the casserole dish on the center rack of the oven. Bake uncovered for about 20 minutes, or until chicken is lightly browned. Baste frequently with the pan juices to keep chicken from becoming dry. While the chicken is baking, prepare the Roasted Pepper Cilantro Sauce Supreme.

Once the chicken is finished baking, remove from the oven. Serve with ½ cup of Roasted Pepper Cilantro Sauce Supreme spooned atop each chicken breast. Any leftover sauce should be used in the next 2–3 days.

Chipotle Chicken and Black Bean Salad

SERVES 6

HONEY-LIME VINAIGRETTE DRESSING

2 tablespoons honey

2 tablespoons Dijon-style mustard

1–2 teaspoons Chipotle-Lime Rub (see page 70)

1 teaspoon Mexican oregano (rub between fingertips to release flavor)

1 teaspoon Key lime zest

¼ cup Key lime juice

½ cup lemon juice

½ cup extra-virgin olive oil

½ teaspoon salt

1 clove garlic, bruised (press with the flat side of a knife until juice is released)

1 tablespoon minced chives

Freshly ground black pepper

CHICKEN

1½ pounds organic boneless, skinless chicken breasts

1–2 tablespoons key lime juice

2 or more tablespoons Chipotle-Lime Rub (see page 70)

1 cup thinly sliced green onions

½ cup minced celery

½ cup finely chopped red bell pepper

½ cup minced cilantro leaves

1 can (15 ounces) black beans, drained and rinsed

¼ cup dried cranberries

If you make the Chipotle-Lime Rub ahead of time, this recipe doesn't take a lot of time. The rub takes about an hour to make but can be used in a variety of recipes. I usually prepare the chicken and dressing the day before or early in the morning of the day that I will be serving the salad. The chicken will be cold and everything can be quickly assembled. The flavorsome balance of black beans, chicken, chipotle, and citrus combined with colorful vegetables is visually appealing and very satisfying.

Combine all the ingredients for the dressing and refrigerate for at least 2 hours.

Rinse the chicken pieces under cold water and pat dry with paper towels. A boneless and skinless chicken breast is not of even thickness and usually has a small piece of breast loosely attached. In order to assure even cooking, detach the small piece.

Place the larger part of the breast between two sheets of wax paper and pound with a meat mallet or the back of a heavy spoon to achieve an even ½-inch thickness. This also breaks up the meat somewhat to allow the rub to penetrate. Place on a nonreactive plate. Repeat this procedure for the remaining chicken pieces.

Sprinkle the chicken breasts with lime juice. Use just enough to moisten both sides. Coat the breasts generously with Chipotle-Lime Rub. Transfer breasts to a nonreactive bowl, cover, and allow to marinate in the refrigerator for 2 hours.

Preheat electric grill or broiler at high heat. Grill or broil the chicken close to the heat source for 3–4 minutes on each side, or

1 Hass avocado, chopped

⅓ cup finely chopped raw pecans

10 cups Earthbound Farm organic herb salad, or mixed baby greens

Calories per serving: 517
Total fat: 25g
Saturated fat: 4g
Calories from fat: 216
Protein: 42g
Carbohydrates: 34g
Dietary fiber: 11g
Sugars: 10g

until slightly browned. The chicken should be juicy in the center but not pink.

For grilling over coals, place the chicken where the coals are the hottest and cook for 3–4 minutes, or until slightly browned. Test a piece by slicing and checking doneness so it isn't overcooked. When done, remove from heat and allow for cooling.

Cut chicken into bite-size pieces, and in a medium-size bowl, combine with the green onions, celery, bell pepper, cilantro, and black beans. Refrigerate until you are ready to serve.

Just before serving, add the cranberries, avocado, and pecans; toss. Add enough of the dressing to generously coat the mixture and toss. Place a serving of salad greens on each plate and top with the chicken mixture. Keep the extra salad dressing available for those who want more.

Lemon-Lime Prickly Pear Chicken

(UNDER 30 MINUTES)
SERVES 6

MARINADE

¼ cup Arizona Cactus Prickly Pear Nectar

⅓ cup extra-virgin olive oil

2 tablespoons Key lime juice

⅓ cup lemon juice

2–4 teaspoons Chipotle-Lime Rub (see page 70)

1 teaspoon Dijon-style mustard

Freshly ground black pepper

½ teaspoon salt

1½–2 pounds organic boneless, skinless chicken breasts

Calories per serving: 235
Total fat: 8g
Saturated fat: 2g
Calories from fat: 71
Protein: 33g
Carbohydrates: 6g
Dietary fiber: 0g
Sugars: 3g

Fuchsia-colored fruit against the green fleshy pads of the prickly pear cactus color the desert during July and August. Native Americans have included the fruits and pads of the prickly pear cactus in their diets for centuries, and our family has also harvested the fruits and turned them into juice for drinks and marinades. This tasty dish is one that we have enjoyed over the years. For convenience, bottled prickly pear nectar (available in many health-oriented grocery stores, either with or without sugar) is used in this recipe. Serve with Southwest Quinoa Pilaf (page 154) or atop fresh salad greens.

Whisk all the marinade ingredients together in a medium-size bowl. If you prefer a very mild marinade with just a hint of chipotle flavor, use only 2 teaspoons of Chipotle-Lime Rub. If you want a bolder flavor with more heat, increase the amount of rub to 4 or more teaspoons. Doing this also increases the salt. Therefore, cut back on the salt, or add salt only after chicken is cooked.

Rinse the chicken breasts under cold water and pat dry with paper towels. Cut the chicken into bite-size pieces and add to the marinade, making sure that pieces are completely coated. Cover and allow to marinate for 2 hours in the refrigerator. Toss the chicken a couple of times while marinating. Soak 12 bamboo skewers in water for 15 minutes near the end of the 2 hours.

After marinating, thread chicken onto the skewers. To ensure even cooking, allow some space between the chicken pieces.

If grilling on a gas or charcoal grill, set at high heat or allow coals to become hot. Place the skewers on the grill and cook until the chicken is browned. Turn and cook on the other side for about 2 minutes, or until chicken is done and moist.

If you broil, preheat the oven to broil at high heat. Place the skewers on the broiler pan as close to the broiler as possible. Allow the chicken to brown slightly. Turn over the chicken pieces and broil until done, 2–3 minutes.

If using an electric grill, set at high heat and grill until browned on one side, about 4 minutes. Turn and grill on the other side until browned or the chicken is done but moist.

Serve immediately, or serve chilled atop a tossed salad.

Poached Chicken and Chicken Broth

MAKES 11 CUPS

1 organic chicken, cut into pieces, or 3 pounds organic chicken breasts with bone

14 cups water

1 celery rib with leaves, cut in thirds

1 medium onion, cut in quarters

1 tablespoon parsley leaves

1 tablespoon sage

1 bay leaf, broken

½ teaspoon salt

BROTH
Calories per serving: 38
Total fat: 1g
Saturated fat: 0g
Calories from fat: 13
Protein: 5g
Carbohydrates: 3g
Dietary fiber: 0g
Sugars: 0g

CHICKEN
Calories per serving: 172
Total fat: 4g
Saturated fat: 1g
Calories from fat: 32
Protein: 32g
Carbohydrates: 0g
Dietary fiber: 0g
Sugars: 0g

Poached chicken can be used in soups, tacos, enchiladas, barbecue, chile relleno stuffing, and much more. The broth from the chicken can be used immediately or stored in the freezer for up to 6 months.

Place all ingredients in a heavy soup pot over high heat. Bring to a boil and then turn heat to low and simmer until chicken is done and will easily come off the bones—about 1 hour. With a slotted spoon, scoop the chicken from broth. Remove the meat from the bones and refrigerate for later use.

To have chicken broth with a wonderfully rich flavor, toss the bones back into the broth and simmer, covered, on low for about 2 more hours. Allow the broth to cool. Strain broth and refrigerate until fat hardens on top of the broth. Defat the chicken broth by removing and discarding the hardened fat.

Pulled Chicken in Seasoned Chicken Broth

SERVES 4

½ cup diced tomatoes

½ cup diced onion

2 cloves garlic, pressed through garlic press

2 cups nonfat organic chicken broth, with or without salt

2 cups shredded or pulled chicken

½ teaspoon oregano (rub between fingertips to release flavor)

½ teaspoon sage (rub between fingertips to release flavor)

1 tablespoon parsley leaves

2 Anaheim or New Mexico green chiles, roasted (see roasting instructions, pages 34–36), or 2 canned green chiles (optional)

Salt

Freshly ground black pepper

Calories per serving: 135
Total fat: 3g
Saturated fat: 1g
Calories from fat: 25
Protein: 23g
Carbohydrates: 4g
Dietary fiber: 1g
Sugars: 2g

"Pulled" chicken is simply poached chicken pulled from the bone and then shredded with two forks. You can enhance the flavor of the chicken by slow-cooking it in its own broth, canned broth, barbecue sauce, or enchilada sauce. Use it in the Flat Enchiladas on page 100, Leftover Fish or Chicken Tacos on page 110, or Leftover Chicken or Tofu Wraps on page 112.

In a small saucepan over medium heat, sauté the tomatoes, onion, and garlic in 1 tablespoon of chicken broth until the onions start to become soft—about 2 minutes. If there is not enough liquid, add another tablespoon of broth.

Add the chicken, broth, oregano, sage, parsley, and green chiles. Bring to a boil over high heat. Turn heat to low, cover, and simmer for about 45 minutes. After simmering, take the lid from the saucepan and allow the broth to evaporate until there is little broth remaining.

Remove from burner and add salt and pepper to taste. Use immediately or refrigerate for up to 2 days.

The chiles will add 7 additional calories and 1g carbohydrates per serving.

Pecan-Crusted Chicken-Yam Roll-Ups

(UNDER 30 MINUTES)
SERVES 6

1½ pounds organic boneless, skinless chicken breasts (3 half-breasts)

Extra-virgin olive oil

2 tablespoons Key lime juice

2 tablespoons Chipotle-Lime Rub (see page 70)

1 medium garnet yam

1 teaspoon extra-virgin olive oil

1 teaspoon Mexican oregano (rub between fingertips to release flavor)

2 tablespoons minced onion

3 tablespoons cilantro leaves

½ cup finely grated goat cheese

2 tablespoons finely chopped dates, or dried organic cranberries (optional)

¼ cup chopped pecans

Extra-virgin olive oil sprayed from oil pump

Calories per serving: 329
Total fat: 15g
Saturated fat: 4g
Calories from fat: 134
Protein: 36g
Carbohydrates: 11g
Dietary fiber: 2g
Sugars: 5g

These roll-ups make a lovely presentation and can be prepared in a short amount of time after marinating. If you want to forego the pecans, they are still delicious! Serve with Spicy Broccoli (page 161) and an Easy Day Salad (page 85).

Preheat oven to 350 degrees F.

Rinse chicken breasts under cold water and pat dry with paper towels. For ease in rolling and for suggested serving size, place each half chicken breast between two pieces of plastic wrap. Using a meat mallet or the back of a heavy spoon, pound each chicken piece to about ⅛ inch thick, or as thin as possible without falling apart. This will ensure marinade absorption and quick even cooking. Spray or rub each piece with olive oil (about 1½ tablespoons), sprinkle with lime juice, and coat with 2 teaspoons of the Chipotle-Lime Rub. Place on a nonreactive plate and marinate for 1 hour in the refrigerator, if you have time. If you are in a hurry, you can just let it marinate while you get everything else ready.

Slice the yam into ¼-inch slices. In a small saucepan, insert a vegetable steamer basket. Add water to just below the basket. Add yam slices and bring to a boil over high heat. Reduce heat, cover, and steam until the slices are crisp, yet tender, about 4 minutes. Remove from heat, drain, and transfer to a plate to limit additional cooking. Cut the slices into strips.

Coat an 8½ x 14 x 2½-inch baking pan with 1 teaspoon of olive oil.

Cover each chicken piece with ¼ cup or more of yam strips and sprinkle with oregano, onion, cilantro, and cheese. Add a few dates or cranberries, if desired.

Roll each piece of chicken so it wraps around the yam filling. Roll the outside of the piece in the pecans and place seam side down in a casserole dish. Arrange so the chicken pieces are not touching in the dish, and bake for approximately 15 minutes on the bottom rack of the oven. To avoid overcooking the chicken, check periodically.

Remove from the oven, spray tops with olive oil, and allow to sit for 5 minutes. Cut each roll in half before serving; serve warm.

Variation—Pecan-Crusted Chicken-Spinach-Yam Roll-Up
SERVES 6

Calories per serving: 317
Total fat: 15g
Saturated fat: 4g
Calories from fat: 134
Protein: 36g
Carbohydrates: 8g
Dietary fiber: 2g
Sugars: 3g

Steam about 3 cups of fresh spinach. Remove when just slightly limp and drain. Substitute steamed spinach for half of the yam filling and eliminate the cilantro.

Variation—Pecan-Crusted Chicken-Spinach Roll-Ups
SERVES 6

Calories per serving: 306
Total fat: 15g
Saturated fat: 4g
Calories from fat: 135
Protein: 36g
Carbohydrates: 5g
Dietary fiber: 2g
Sugars: 2g

Steam about 6 cups of fresh spinach. Remove when just slightly limp and drain. Replace the yams with steamed spinach. Also eliminate the oregano and cilantro. Add 1 tablespoon of minced red bell peppers.

Variation—Pecan-Crusted Chicken-Black Bean Roll-Ups

SERVES 6

Calories per serving: 353
Total fat: 16g
Saturated fat: 4g
Calories from fat: 136
Protein: 40g
Carbohydrates: 13g
Dietary fiber: 5g
Sugars: 1g

Use the same ingredients and follow the same directions as in the Pecan-Crusted Chicken-Yam Roll-Ups on page 140, but make the following changes. Substitute about 1½ cups (¼ cup per roll-up) of drained and rinsed canned black beans for the yams and eliminate the cranberries and/or dates. Add 2 Anaheim or New Mexico roasted green chiles (see roasting instructions, pages 34–36), or canned green chiles (cut to create 1 strip per roll-up), and 1 minced garlic clove (⅙ clove per roll-up).

Southwest Turkeyloaf

SERVES 8

LOAF

1 can (15 ounces) pinto beans

5 thick (or 7 thin) corn tortillas

1 pound lean ground turkey

1 bag (6 ounces) baby spinach, chopped, or 2 packages (10 ounces each) frozen spinach

¼ cup tomato paste

½ cup minced celery

½ cup minced cilantro leaves, packed

⅓ cup organic golden flaxmeal

1 teaspoon Mexican oregano

½ teaspoon ground cumin

1 teaspoon New Mexico red chile powder (mild, medium, or hot)

5 cloves garlic, pressed through garlic press

2 green chiles, roasted and minced (see pages 34–36), or 1 can (4 ounces) diced green chiles

Enjoy this international meatloaf, where flavors from north and south of the border are brought together to wake up your taste buds. Kristina Beckman Brito and family tested this recipe and rated it as very satisfying and easy to prepare. The next morning for breakfast, she scrambled some of the leftovers with eggs, rolled it up in whole-grain tortillas, and enjoyed. It's a much better choice than most cereals or waffles! Serve with Lemon-Vinaigrette Green Bean and Yam Salad (page 165).

Preheat oven to 350 degrees F.

Drain the beans and reserve the juice. In a large bowl, mash the beans with a vegetable masher. Add enough bean juice to render a lumpy, creamy mixture. Set aside.

Cut the tortillas into fourths and place in a food processor. Process into coarse crumbs. This should yield 1¾ cups of crumbs. Add crumbs and all other loaf ingredients (except for the olive

1 medium yellow onion, minced

Extra-virgin olive oil

CREAMY TOPPING

1 cup organic soft tofu, drained

⅓ cup low-sodium, nonfat
organic chicken broth

½ cup finely chopped
yellow onion

2 cloves garlic, pressed
through garlic press

½ cup grated Soy-Sation
premium mozzarella soy cheese

⅓ cup grated Soy-Sation lite
pepper Jack soy cheese

SAUCE

1¼ cups Roasted
Red Bell Pepper Chipotle
Enchilada Sauce (see page 99),
or use canned Rosarita or
Hatch enchilada sauce

1 can (15 ounces) chopped
tomatoes, drained, or 2 large
fresh tomatoes, chopped

1 cup thinly sliced green onions

1 large red bell pepper, roasted
and coarsely chopped (see
roasting instructions,
pages 34–36)

¼ cup sliced black olives

¼ cup chopped cilantro

Calories per serving: 302
Total fat: 8g
Saturated fat: 1g
Calories from fat: 70
Protein: 23g
Carbohydrates: 38g
Dietary fiber: 10g
Sugars: 9g

oil) to the beans. (If you are using frozen spinach, you will first need to let it thaw and squeeze the water out of it.) Mix with your hands until thoroughly blended.

Spray a 12 x 7½ x 2-inch glass casserole dish with olive oil. Place the turkeyloaf mixture into the casserole dish and shape into a loaf. Make an indention on top, almost the entire length of the loaf, about 1 inch deep and 3 inches wide. Bake uncovered for 50 minutes.

While the turkeyloaf is baking, cream the tofu and chicken broth in a blender until smooth. Pour the creamed mixture into a mixing bowl and mix with onion, garlic, and soy cheeses.

Remove the loaf from the oven and fill the indention with the soy-cheese mixture. Pour enchilada sauce and tomatoes over the entire loaf. Cover and bake for another 15 minutes.

Remove the loaf from the oven. Sprinkle with green onions, bell pepper, olives, and cilantro. Let the loaf sit for 5 minutes before serving. Slice into 8 equal portions and serve.

Agustín's Skillet

(UNDER 30 MINUTES)
SERVES 6

1–1½ pounds lean ground turkey

1 teaspoon extra-virgin olive oil

1 teaspoon oregano (rub between fingertips to release flavor)

5 cloves garlic, pressed through garlic press

1½ cups chopped fresh tomatoes

1 large onion, sliced

½ head green cabbage, shredded with a knife

2 cups snap peas or snow peas

1 Anaheim or New Mexico green chile, seeds and veins removed, chopped

1 red bell pepper, seeds removed, chopped

1 yellow bell pepper, seeds removed, chopped

2 tablespoons whole-grain flour

¼ cup water, or as needed

¼ cup chopped cilantro

1–2 teaspoons red chile flakes (optional)

Sea salt

Freshly ground black pepper

Calories per serving: 366
Total fat: 12g
Saturated fat: 3g
Calories from fat: 103
Protein: 26g
Carbohydrates: 40g
Dietary fiber: 7g
Sugars: 6g

My husband, Agustín, came up with this family favorite. "Comfort food" is the phrase that our friends believe best represents this dish. The no-stress preparation can usually be accomplished in under 30 minutes. Serve over whole-grain rice, quinoa, or couscous, or with corn tortillas. Cut the carbs and eat it without any grains—it's delicious! Our children used to enjoy the leftovers rolled up in whole-grain flour tortillas for their school lunches.

In a 5-quart saucepan, over medium heat, sauté the turkey in the olive oil until almost done. Add oregano, garlic, tomatoes, onions, and cabbage, and sauté for about 5 minutes. Toss in the peas, green chile, and red and yellow bell peppers. Cook until the vegetables are crisp, yet tender, and brightly colored, about 4 minutes.

In a small bowl, mix the flour with enough water to render a smooth mixture. Add to the saucepan juices and stir to thicken the juices.

Remove from heat. Gently fold in the cilantro. For a spicy-hot flavor, add red chile flakes. If necessary, add a little salt and pepper. If desired, present each serving over ½ cup whole-grain rice, couscous, quinoa, or a corn tortilla.

10

CHAPTER

Southwest Specialties

Chile-Lime Tofu

SERVES 4

1 pound extra-firm organic tofu

1 tablespoon extra-virgin olive oil

2 tablespoons lemon juice

1 tablespoon maple syrup

½ teaspoon Dijon-style mustard

1–2 tablespoons Chipotle-Lime Rub (see page 70)

Lemon juice

1 bag (6 ounces) spinach

Calories per serving: 172
Total fat: 10g
Saturated fat: 1g
Calories from fat: 87
Protein: 13g
Carbohydrates: 11g
Dietary fiber: 1g
Sugars: 7g

Chipotle-Lime Rub makes this recipe. The combination of citrus, chipotle, tofu, and wilted spinach elicits satisfying flavors and textures. The rub takes a little bit of preparation time, but it can be used and enjoyed in a number of recipes throughout the cookbook and keeps well refrigerated for up to 2 months. This dish is slow-cooked, which firms up the tofu and bakes in the flavors. Soy (aside from highly refined soy products) may have numerous health benefits—from reducing the risk of cardiovascular disease and some cancers to mitigating the ills of menopause.

Drain the water off the block of tofu and cut it into ½-inch cubes or smaller. Expel water from the cubes by placing them in a single layer on a large plate. Cover with wax paper and place a large cast-iron skillet or other heavy flat object on top of the wax paper. Drain for ½ hour and remove water from the plate as it accumulates.

Whisk together olive oil, lemon juice, maple syrup, and mustard. Place the drained tofu cubes in a small dish that can that can go from the refrigerator directly to the oven; pour the marinade over the cubes and toss. Generously coat the cubes with the Chipotle-Lime Rub and marinate in the refrigerator for 4–24 hours.

After marinating, do not drain the tofu. Set the oven at 250 degrees F and bake for 1 hour. Add more lemon juice to the casserole dish as needed to keep juices from burning. To achieve a firmer tofu, reduce temperature to 200 degrees F and bake for an additional hour, or until the desired firmness is achieved.

Remove from the oven and add the fresh spinach to the casserole dish; toss with the tofu and juices, causing the spinach to slightly wilt. Serve immediately.

Chipotle Barbecue Tofu and Vegetables

SERVES 4

1 pound organic extra-firm tofu

⅔ cup Annie's Naturals Organic BBQ Hot Chipotle, or Arizona's Finest Chipotle BBQ Sauce

1⅓ cups low-sodium nonfat organic chicken broth

½ red bell pepper, chopped

½ poblano pepper, chopped

⅓ cup chopped yellow onion

1 small yellow squash, coarsely chopped

½ cup chopped cilantro

Calories per serving: 153
Total fat: 7g
Saturated fat: 1g
Calories from fat: 58
Protein: 12g
Carbohydrates: 12g
Dietary fiber: 2g
Sugars: 7g

"Barbecued" tofu offers a tasty alternative to a meat or chicken barbecue dish. Tofu is like a sponge, soaking up that wonderful barbecue flavor. As a plus, its protein quality is very close to animal protein but without the saturated fat. Like meat, soy contains all the amino acids that the body requires, making it a complete protein. To give this dish a little chicken flavor, chicken broth is added to the sauce.

Preheat oven to 350 degrees F. Drain the water off the tofu and cut it into ½-inch cubes. Expel water from the cubes by placing them in a single layer on a large plate. Cover with wax paper and place a large cast-iron skillet or other heavy flat object on top of the wax paper. Drain for approximately 1 hour and remove water from the plate as it accumulates.

Mix the barbecue sauce and chicken broth together in a bowl. Place the tofu cubes in a casserole dish in a single layer. The container should be just big enough for the tofu cubes. Pour the sauce over the cubes and toss to completely coat with the sauce. If there is not enough sauce to completely cover the cubes, add enough chicken broth to cover. Place in the oven and bake for 50 minutes.

Remove from the oven, add all other ingredients, and then toss. Spoon over quinoa, brown rice, or whole-grain couscous, or wrap in a sprouted whole-grain wheat tortilla.

Sun-Dried Tomato Focaccia Bread

SERVES 8

1 cup boiling water

12 sun-dried tomatoes

1¼ cups lukewarm water

2 teaspoons active-dry yeast

1⅓ cups unbleached all-purpose flour

2 cups stone-ground whole wheat flour

1½ teaspoons salt

3 tablespoons extra-virgin olive oil

3 medium cloves garlic, pressed through garlic press

2 tablespoons fresh rosemary

2 teaspoons extra-virgin olive oil

Calories per serving: 174
Total fat: 6g
Saturated fat: 1g
Calories from fat: 50
Protein: 5g
Carbohydrates: 26g
Dietary fiber: 4g
Sugars: 0g

This is a family recipe from Nicole Barry's grandmother, whose heritage and cooking are Italian. I altered it by adding sun-dried tomatoes and whole-grain flour. You will love it! If you use an oil pump sprayer for the olive oil, you will use less oil.

Preheat the oven to 425 degrees F. Pour 1 cup of boiling water over the sun-dried tomatoes and soak for 10 minutes. Drain and gently squeeze to remove any excess water. Stir yeast into the lukewarm water in a small bowl and let it sit for 5 minutes.

Meanwhile, in the work bowl of a food processor, process the all-purpose and whole wheat flours, salt, 3 tablespoons of olive oil, garlic, rosemary, and drained sun-dried tomatoes until the tomatoes are minced. With machine running, pour the yeast water through the feed tube in a steady stream into the flour mixture. Process until the dough forms a ball—about 1 minute. If the dough appears to be too wet and all the dough doesn't come together to form a ball, continue to process, adding small amounts of flour, until the dough forms a ball.

Coat a large glass bowl with the other 2 teaspoons of olive oil. Oil your hands with olive oil and remove the dough from the work bowl. Form the dough into a ball and place it in the oiled bowl. Cover with a damp cloth. Allow dough to rise until almost doubled, 1½–2 hours.

Coat a 15 x 10 x 1-inch jellyroll pan with olive oil.

Gently deflate the dough with your finger. Transfer the dough to the jellyroll pan and press to fit into the pan. Cover with a damp cloth that has been sprayed with olive oil. Allow the dough to rise again until almost double, 1–1½ hours.

Lightly spray the dough with olive oil. Bake until the top is lightly toasted, about 20 minutes. Cut into 8 serving slices and serve fresh from the oven or cooled.

Southwest Pizza

(UNDER 30 MINUTES)
SERVES 8

1 teaspoon extra-virgin olive oil

1 Sun-Dried Tomato Focaccia Bread recipe (see page 149), or Alvarado Street sprouted pizza bread, or other whole-grain unbaked or ready-to-eat crust

1 tablespoon fresh rosemary

2 cloves garlic, pressed through garlic press

8 basil leaves, finely torn

½ cup thinly sliced zucchini

½ cup thinly sliced crookneck squash

½ cup coarsely chopped, deveined red bell pepper

1⅔ tablespoons extra-virgin olive oil

2 Anaheim or New Mexico green chiles, roasted, peeled, deveined, and chopped (see pages 34–36), or 2 canned green chiles

1 cup chopped roasted eggplant or sweet potato (see pages 34–37)

2 Applegate Farms roasted red bell pepper organic sausages, or 1 low-fat chipotle chile chicken sausage, cut into bite-size pieces

7 thin onion slices

¼ cup crumbled goat feta cheese

¼ cup raw piñons

You won't find a pizza healthier than this one. The Sun-Dried Tomato Focaccia Bread is delicious, but does take time to prepare. Other commercial alternatives are available, which will add less stress to your life on a busy day and be just as healthy. We recommend Alvarado Street sprouted pizza bread, available at health-oriented grocery stores; other brands are also available. Read the labels for whole-grain options with no oil or with olive or canola oil.

Preheat oven to 350 degrees F.

Rub 1 teaspoon of olive oil over the focaccia or pizza bread, then rub on the rosemary and garlic, and sprinkle on the basil.

In a medium bowl, toss the zucchini, crookneck squash, and red bell pepper in the remaining olive oil.

Layer the green chiles and roasted eggplant or sweet potato on top of the seasoned crust, and then add the uncooked squash mixture. Top off with the sausage pieces, onion, feta cheese, and raw piñons.

Bake for about 10 minutes or until the pizza is hot in the middle and the vegetables are slightly cooked.

½ **Hass avocado, sliced, peeled, and chopped**

2 Key limes, quartered

Calories per serving: 327
Total fat: 13g
Saturated fat: 2g
Calories from fat: 108
Protein: 12g
Carbohydrates: 43g
Dietary fiber: 3g
Sugars: 3g

Remove from the oven and cool for 5 minutes. Scatter avocado pieces over the top and squeeze lime juice over the avocado. Cut into 8 pieces and serve warm.

Spicy Spinach Pizza

(UNDER 30 MINUTES)
SERVES 8

¾ **cup crumbled, drained firm tofu**

4 cloves garlic, pressed through garlic press

3 tablespoons minced fresh basil leaves

Salt

½ **cup grated Soy-Sation Pepper Jack soy cheese**

2 packages (10 ounces each) frozen chopped spinach, thawed, with water squeezed out

1 whole-grain or sprouted grain 12-inch focaccia bread, or Sun-Dried Tomato Focaccia Bread (see page 149)

1 teaspoon extra-virgin olive oil

1 tablespoon fresh rosemary leaves, bruised (press with the flat side of a knife until juice is released)

(continued)

This has always been a winner among our children and their friends. Whenever Elicia invited her sorority sister, Nicole Barry, to our house for dinner, Nicole would call in advance and ask me to make the Spicy Spinach Pizza. Today, my daughter makes it for her three-year-old son, Ty. We both usually use Alvarado Street sprouted pizza bread from a health-oriented grocery store. If you have time, freeze a tub of firm tofu (not silken) the day before you want to make this recipe; you can thaw it in the closed tub in 10 minutes under hot water. When frozen tofu is thawed, squeezing tofu between your hands easily squeezes the water out. It also crumbles better than tofu that has not been frozen. If you don't have frozen tofu, you can use either silken or regular tofu, but it needs to be drained first.

Preheat oven to 350 degrees F.

Crumble the tofu and thoroughly mix with half of the garlic, the basil, a pinch of salt, the soy cheese, and the spinach. If possible, allow this mixture to sit for 1 hour so the flavors blend.

½ cup crumbled
goat feta cheese

½ cup chopped red onion

½ red bell pepper, sliced

1 medium tomato, chopped
or thinly sliced

1 can (4 ounces)
sliced black olives

1 teaspoon extra-virgin olive oil

Calories per serving: 400
Total fat: 10g
Saturated fat: 1g
Calories from fat: 83
Protein: 9g
Carbohydrates: 43g
Dietary fiber: 3g
Sugars: 2g

If you are making the Sun-Dried Tomato Focaccia bread, after it is baked, cut off approximately a 12 x 10-inch piece for the pizza. Coat the top of the crust with 1 teaspoon of olive oil and rub with the remaining garlic and the bruised rosemary; cover with the spinach mixture. Sprinkle the spinach with feta cheese and top with onion, bell pepper, tomato, and olives.

Place the pizza directly on a rack in the middle of the oven and bake for about 8 minutes, or until topping is heated through and the cheeses are melted. Don't overcook, because the soy cheese will turn rubbery.

After baking, drizzle 1 teaspoon of olive oil over the topping and let sit for 5 minutes. Cut into 8 pieces and serve.

11
CHAPTER

Side Dishes

Southwest Quinoa Pilaf

SERVES 6

½ poblano pepper

½ red bell pepper

1 small crookneck squash

4 large garlic cloves

1 cup boiling water

6 sun-dried tomatoes

1 cup quinoa

2 cups nonfat organic chicken broth, with or without salt

½ –1 teaspoon New Mexico red chile powder (mild, medium, or hot), or Chipotle-Lime Rub (see page 70)

¼ teaspoon ground cumin

½ teaspoon oregano (rub between fingertips to release flavor)

2 teaspoons extra-virgin olive oil

½ cup finely sliced green onions (include some green)

1 cup cooked black beans, drained and rinsed

½ cup minced cilantro leaves

⅛ teaspoon salt (eliminate if there is salt in the chicken broth)

Freshly ground black pepper

¼ cup piñons

Calories per serving: 238
Total fat: 9g
Saturated fat: 1g
Calories from fat: 79
Protein: 9g
Carbohydrates: 33g
Dietary fiber: 9g
Sugars: 3g

Once you try gluten-free Southwest Quinoa Pilaf with its rich, nutty flavor, you may never go back to traditional rice. Quinoa is a complete protein, supplying all the essential amino acids in balanced form. The added beans and vegetables make this a one-dish meal! Some brands of quinoa need to be rinsed to remove the bitter shell that may remain on the grain. I've used the Ancient Harvest and Trader Joe's brands and have not had to rinse either one.

Roast the poblano and bell peppers, squash, and garlic (follow the directions on pages 34–38), then peel and finely chop them (you don't need to peel the squash). Pour the boiling water over the sun-dried tomatoes and soak for 10–15 minutes. Drain and finely chop after rehydrating.

Place the quinoa in a small bowl and add enough water to cover. Swish it around a bit, then drain. You may have to do this a couple of times. When the water runs clear, the quinoa should be ready to use. You may also put the quinoa in an ultra-fine strainer and run water over it. (If the strainer isn't fine enough, the quinoa will slip through the holes.)

In a medium saucepan, mix together the quinoa, chicken broth, chile powder or Chipotle-Lime Rub, cumin, and oregano; bring to a boil over high heat, then turn to low heat and simmer for 10–15 minutes, or until the grain has soaked up the broth. Remove from the burner and place in an appropriate-sized bowl; toss with olive oil. Immediately add all other ingredients, including the roasted vegetables, and toss. Serve warm.

Butternut Squash Couscous

SERVES 6

1 small butternut squash, 5–6 inches in length

Extra-virgin olive oil

½ cup finely chopped green onions

2 cloves garlic, pressed through garlic press

1½ cups low-sodium, nonfat organic chicken broth

½ teaspoon New Mexico red chile powder (mild, medium, or hot)

¼ teaspoon nutmeg

½ teaspoon ground cinnamon

½ cup fresh or frozen peas

1 cup prepared whole-grain couscous

1 tablespoon organic tamari soy sauce (low-sodium)

¼ cup sun-dried raisins or chopped dates

2 tablespoons chopped cilantro

¼ cup finely chopped hulled pumpkin seeds

Calories per serving: 215
Total fat: 4g
Saturated fat: 1g
Calories from fat: 33
Protein: 7g
Carbohydrates: 40g
Dietary fiber: 3g
Sugars: 7g

The fall season brings luscious colors of winter squash, which Native Americans and other peoples of the Southwest have used as a staple for centuries. My friend Maryetta Patch, who grew up on the Fort Mojave Reservation, recalls her grandmother preparing stews and dessert dishes from various types of squash and toasting the seeds to be used in recipes or eaten as a snack.

Preheat oven to 350 degrees F.

Peel the butternut squash with a vegetable peeler, scoop out the seeds, and cut the meat of the squash into tiny cubes. Coat a 14 x 7 x 2-inch baking pan with olive oil. Place the squash in the pan and toss with additional olive oil. Bake for approximately 15 minutes. Remove from the oven and add the onions and garlic. Toss together with a spatula, return to the oven, and continue baking for approximately 5 minutes longer, or until the squash can be penetrated with the tines of a fork.

In a 2-quart saucepan, place the chicken broth, chile powder, nutmeg, and cinnamon; bring to a boil. Add the peas, reduce to medium heat, and cook for 6–8 minutes or until the peas are done. Remove from the burner and stir in the couscous, soy sauce, and the squash mixture. Cover and allow to sit for 10 minutes. Uncover, add raisins or dates, cilantro, and pumpkin seeds; fluff the couscous with a fork to mix. Serve immediately.

Mexican Corn on the Cob

(UNDER 30 MINUTES)
SERVES 4

4 average-size ears of corn

2 Key limes, halved

**New Mexico red chile powder
(mild, medium, or hot)**

Salt

Freshly ground black pepper

Calories per serving: 157
Total fat: 2g
Saturated fat: 0g
Calories from fat: 54
Protein: 4g
Carbohydrates: 32g
Dietary fiber: 3g
Sugars: 1g

Roasted corn, commonly sold by street vendors in Mexico, is deli-cious with a little bit of lime, chile powder, and a dash of salt. Unlike corn on the cob in the U.S., it is not drenched in butter. Sweet corn is in season during the summer, you'll get the best flavor and sweetness when you can buy it at a farmers market.

Peel and clean the ears of corn

Preset the grill or broiler to high heat. Place the ears as close to the heat source as possible and roast until the kernels become somewhat browned. Remove from heat. Squeeze lime juice over the kernels, sprinkle with chile powder, and add a little salt and pepper.

Gala Butternut Squash with Green Beans

SERVES 4

2 small butternut squash (larger ones will be difficult to peel)

3 teaspoons extra-virgin olive oil

2 cups fresh green beans, trimmed and cut in half diagonally

2 cloves garlic, pressed through garlic press

1 large tomato, chopped

½ cup sliced red onion

¼ cup minced poblano pepper

1 red bell pepper, coarsely chopped

1–2 teaspoons extra-virgin olive oil

2 tablespoons lemon juice

⅛ teaspoon nutmeg

⅛ teaspoon ground cardamom

⅛ teaspoon ground cinnamon

¼ teaspoon turmeric

Pinch of sea salt

Freshly ground black pepper

3 tablespoons chopped hulled pumpkin seeds

Calories per serving: 103
Total fat: 3g
Saturated fat: 1g
Calories from fat: 28
Protein: 3g
Carbohydrates: 18g
Dietary fiber: 5g
Sugars: 6g

The vivid colors in this medley of fruit and vegetables bring festive colors to the table, and their complementary flavors bring pleasure to the palate—not to mention the rewarding health aspects of this combination.

Preheat the oven to 350 degrees F. Using a vegetable peeler, peel the squash. Cut it in half, lengthwise, and scoop out the stringy meat and seeds. Slice the squash and cut into small chunks or cubes.

Coat the sides and bottom of an 11 x 7 x 2-inch casserole dish with 1 teaspoon of the olive oil. Add the squash to the casserole dish and coat with the other 2 teaspoons of the olive oil. During baking, turn the squash pieces a few times; more olive oil may be needed to prevent the squash from sticking. Bake uncovered for 15–20 minutes, or until squash can be penetrated with fork tines. In a medium-size pot, insert a vegetable steamer basket; add water to just below the basket, then add the beans and bring to a boil over high heat. Reduce the heat, cover, and steam for about 4 minutes, or until the beans are bright green and crisp, yet tender. Remove from heat, drain, and transfer to a plate to limit additional cooking.

After the squash is done, mix in the garlic and tomato and bake for an additional 3 minutes, or until tomatoes are a bit soft. Remove from the oven and immediately mix in the onion and poblano and bell pepper. The heat will slightly cook the vegetables.

Sprinkle with 1–2 teaspoons of olive oil, lemon juice, nutmeg, cardamom, cinnamon, turmeric, salt, and pepper; toss to mix. Fold the beans into the squash mixture. Sprinkle with chopped pumpkin seeds. Serve immediately.

Variation—Gala Butternut Squash with Spinach
SERVES 4

Calories per serving: 150
Total fat: 4g
Saturated fat: 1g
Calories from fat: 33
Protein: 6g
Carbohydrates: 28g
Dietary fiber: 6g
Sugars: 12g

Eliminate the green beans and follow the directions for Gala Butternut Squash with Green Beans, up through the step where the onions and garlic are added. In addition to adding the onions and garlic, fold in 2 five-ounce packages of freshly washed baby spinach. Then add the 1–2 teaspoons of olive oil, lemon juice, and the spices. The heat will wilt the spinach and slightly cook the other vegetables. Just before serving, sprinkle the top with ⅓ cup dried cranberries and the pumpkin seeds.

Variation—Gala Butternut Squash with Fresh Basil
SERVES 4

Calories per serving: 88
Total fat: 3g
Saturated fat: 1g
Calories from fat: 28
Protein: 2g
Carbohydrates: 15g
Dietary fiber: 3g
Sugars: 5g

Eliminate the green beans and follow the directions for Gala Butternut Squash with Green Beans, up through the step where the onions and garlic are added. In addition to adding the onions and garlic, add 2 cups of julienned basil leaves. Then add the 1–2 teaspoons of olive oil, lemon juice, and spices; toss to mix. The heat will wilt the basil and slightly cook the other vegetables. Just before serving, sprinkle with pumpkin seeds.

Variation—Gala Butternut Squash with Fresh Cilantro and Chipotle
SERVES 4

Calories per serving: 112
Total fat: 4g
Saturated fat: 1g
Calories from fat: 32
Protein: 4g
Carbohydrates: 20g
Dietary fiber: 5g
Sugars: 6g

Follow the directions for Gala Butternut Squash with Green Beans, but omit the salt. Instead, prior to baking the squash, add 1–2 tablespoons of Chipotle-Lime Rub (see page 70). Also add ½ cup of chopped cilantro leaves at the same time the green beans are added.

Spicy Broccoli

(UNDER 30 MINUTES)
SERVES 6

1 teaspoon extra-virgin olive oil

3 cloves garlic, pressed through garlic press

1 medium onion, chopped

1 red bell pepper, julienned

¼–½ cup dry white wine

1 teaspoon dry mustard powder or Dijon-style mustard

1–2 teaspoons New Mexico red chile powder (adjust for spicy-hot flavor)

4 cups broccoli florets

2 tablespoons julienne-cut basil leaves

1 tablespoon minced cilantro leaves

1 tablespoon Key lime juice

1 tablespoon freshly grated Parmesan cheese (optional)

Pinch of sea salt

Freshly ground black pepper

Calories per serving: 84
Total fat: 2g
Saturated fat: 0g
Calories from fat: 15
Protein: 4g
Carbohydrates: 4g
Dietary fiber: 4g
Sugars: 4g

Since broccoli contains an abundance of health-promoting micro-nutrients, we usually eat broccoli or broccoli sprouts at least three times a week. Steamed is my favorite, but this spicy alternative makes for some tasty variety.

Add olive oil to a large skillet. Place over medium heat and sauté the garlic, onion, and bell pepper for about 5 minutes or until vegetables are crisp, yet tender. Remove from heat and transfer into a serving bowl.

In the same skillet, whisk together ¼ cup of wine with the mustard and chile powder. Place over medium heat. Add broccoli and sauté for about 4 minutes, or until the broccoli is crisp, tender, and bright green. Add more wine as needed for sautéing.

Remove broccoli from heat and transfer to the serving bowl containing the other vegetables. Mix in the basil, cilantro, lime juice, cheese, salt, and pepper. Serve warm.

Adding the Parmesan cheese adds 5 calories and less than ½g of fat per serving.

Steamed Broccoli Tossed in Garlic

(UNDER 30 MINUTES)
SERVES 4

5 garlic cloves

½ red bell pepper

4 cups broccoli florets

1 tablespoon lemon juice

Pinch of sea salt

Freshly ground black pepper

Calories per serving: 44
Total fat: 0g
Saturated fat: 0g
Calories from fat: 0
Protein: 3g
Carbohydrates: 9g
Dietary fiber: 4g
Sugars: 2g

Garlic lovers will enjoy this simple side dish with a tangy flavor. The red bell pepper adds color and, of course, added color brings added micro-nutrients.

Roast, peel, and chop the garlic (see roasting instructions, pages 34–37) ; set aside. Thinly slice the red bell pepper; set aside.

Rinse the broccoli, and trim the stalks to within 1 inch of the florets. Separate the florets into bite-size pieces.

In a large saucepan, insert a vegetable steamer basket and add water to just below the basket. Add broccoli and bring to a boil over high heat. Reduce the heat, cover, and steam for about 4 minutes, or until the broccoli is bright green and crisp, yet tender. Remove from heat, drain, and immediately transfer to a serving bowl to limit additional cooking.

Pour fresh lemon juice over the broccoli, toss in the garlic and bell pepper, and add a pinch of salt and pepper. Toss and serve immediately.

Tangy Cilantro Vegetables

(UNDER 30 MINUTES)
SERVES 4

1 red bell pepper, roasted (see roasting instructions, pages 34–36)

1 poblano pepper, roasted (see roasting instructions, pages 34–36)

1 teaspoon extra-virgin olive oil

2 large cloves garlic, pressed though garlic press

½ cup chopped red onion

3 cups cauliflower florets

1½ cups baby carrots, halved lengthwise

2 tablespoons lemon juice

½ teaspoon lemon zest

1 tablespoon red wine vinegar

½ cup chopped cilantro

Pinch of sea salt

Freshly ground black pepper

Calories per serving: 83
Total fat: 2g
Saturated fat: 0g
Calories from fat: 16
Protein: 3g
Carbohydrates: 16g
Dietary fiber: 5g
Sugars: 8g

A splattering of colorful vegetables against the snow-white cauliflower is as flavorful as it is attractive. This medley of color is full of fiber and micro-nutrients, essential in a health-promoting diet.

After roasting the red bell and poblano peppers, peel them, remove the seeds and veins, and chop. Place in a medium-size serving bowl. Set aside.

Place the olive oil in a small skillet over medium heat. Sauté the garlic and onion for 5 minutes, or until crisp, yet tender. Remove from the burner and scrape the sauté into the serving bowl containing the peppers.

Pour about 2 inches of water into a large saucepan. Place a steaming basket filled with cauliflower and carrots in the pan; cover with lid. Over high heat, bring water to a boil. Turn heat to low and steam vegetables for about 8 minutes, or until the cauliflower stems can be penetrated with fork tines.

Remove vegetables from the saucepan and add to the sauté, along with lemon juice, zest, vinegar, cilantro, salt, and pepper; toss gently. Serve immediately.

Lemon-Vinaigrette Green Bean and Yam Salad

SERVES 4

DRESSING

2 tablespoons lemon juice

2 tablespoons extra-virgin olive oil

2 teaspoons Dijon-style mustard

1 teaspoon honey

¼ cup diced green onion

1 clove garlic, pressed through garlic press

¼ cup minced fresh dill weed

¼ cup chopped cilantro

5 basil leaves, torn

¼ cup crumbled goat feta cheese

SALAD

1 teaspoon extra-virgin olive oil

2 medium-size red garnet yams

1 medium red-skin new potato

2 tablespoons extra-virgin olive oil

1 pound fresh green beans

1 cup coarsely chopped red bell pepper

½ cup diced red onion

3 cloves garlic, pressed through garlic press

Calories per serving: 278
Total fat: 7g
Saturated fat: 2g
Calories from fat: 58
Protein: 7g
Carbohydrates: 52g
Dietary fiber: 11g
Sugars: 9g

This is a beautifully colored "potato salad" with outstanding flavor. As another healthy alternative, substitute bright green, slightly steamed broccoli for the green beans. Broccoli is a premier vegetable full of antioxidants. This dish is delicious hot or cold!

Preheat oven to 350 degrees F. Prepare dressing by combining all dressing ingredients; set aside.

Coat a 14 x 9 x 2½ -inch baking dish with olive oil (about 1 teaspoon). Scrub the yams and red potato. Remove any dark spots and root hair, and cut into ¼-inch slices. Place in baking dish and toss with about 2 tablespoons of olive oil. Bake for 20 minutes.

While yams and potatoes are baking, rinse green beans, trim the ends, and cut in half on a diagonal. In a medium-size pot, insert a vegetable steamer basket; add water to just below the basket. Add beans and bring to a boil over high heat. Reduce heat, cover, and steam for approximately 4 minutes, or until beans are bright green and crisp, yet tender. Remove from heat, drain, and transfer to a plate to prevent additional cooking, then add the red bell pepper and red onion.

Remove yams or sweet potatoes from the oven and add the 3 cloves of pressed garlic; toss with a spatula and bake for a couple of minutes longer or until the tines of a fork can penetrate the potatoes. Remove from oven.

Add the green bean mixture and dressing to the yams or sweet potatoes and mix thoroughly. Serve immediately.

Roasted Portobello Mushrooms and Vegetables

SERVES 6

2 large portobello mushrooms

1 small crookneck squash

1 small zucchini squash

1 large red bell pepper

2 Anaheim or New Mexico green chiles

1 bulb garlic

1 medium eggplant

1 large yam (optional)

1 onion

½ cup chopped basil

1 teaspoon oregano

Salt and freshly ground pepper

2–3 tablespoons extra-virgin olive oil

Sprinkling of goat feta cheese

Calories per serving: 167
Total fat: 7g
Saturated fat: 2g
Calories from fat: 65
Protein: 6g
Carbohydrates: 22g
Dietary fiber: 7g
Sugars: 8g

It may take a little while to roast all of these vegetables, but it is well worth the time. The roasting develops their flavors while retaining their firmness for a wonderful texture and taste. Think of the variety of vegetables you are getting in one meal. Leftover grilled vegetables are great for sandwiches with a little chicken, tofu, or a small amount of goat cheese. Wrap them in a corn or flour tortilla, stuff them in enchiladas or quesadillas, and accent with goat or soy cheese.

Roast the mushrooms, crookneck and zucchini squash, bell pepper, green chiles, garlic, eggplant, yam, and onion (see roasting instructions, pages 34–38). After roasting, peel the bell peppers and chiles; coarsely chop the red bell pepper and finely chop the green chiles. Peel and mince the garlic cloves. Coarsely cut all the other vegetables. Combine the vegetables, seasonings, and olive oil; toss to mix. Top with goat feta cheese.

CHAPTER

12

Desserts

Chocolate Fruit Tart

SERVES 8

CRUST

½ teaspoon butter

½ cup golden flaxseed

6 whole organic
graham crackers

1 tablespoon sugar

½ teaspoon ground ginger

3 tablespoons unrefined
macadamia oil

1 tablespoon water

FILLING

1 Decadent Chocolate Pudding
recipe (see page 172)

TOPPING

½ cup sliced strawberries

1 kiwifruit, peeled and sliced

½ cup blueberries or
blackberries

Calories per serving: 307
Total fat: 15g
Saturated fat: 4g
Calories from fat: 174
Protein: 10g
Carbohydrates: 27g
Dietary fiber: 5g
Sugars: 26g

If you are going to eat a fruit tart, you might as well make the crust as healthy as feasible by using unrefined macadamia oil (high in monounsaturated fat) and ground flaxseed; both contain Omega-3 EFAs. This tart is made with the Decadent Chocolate Pudding, but the Lime Pudding on page 174 is another delicious alternative (omit the raspberries if you use the Lime Pudding recipe).

Preheat oven to 350 degrees F. Coat a 9-inch removable-bottom tart pan, or three 4½-inch mini tart pans, with butter. Grind the flaxseeds in a spice grinder or blender until they become a fine meal.

In a food processor work bowl, combine the flaxmeal, graham crackers, sugar, and ginger until they reach the consistency of fine crumbs. Remove from the food processor; thoroughly mix in the macadamia oil and the tablespoon of water.

With oiled fingertips, firmly press the crumb mixture into the tart pan or pans, making the sides about ¼ inch thick; bake on the middle rack of the oven for about 10 minutes, or until the crust is firm and slightly browned. Remove from the oven and cool before filling with the pudding. (You can prepare the pudding filling while the crust is cooling.)

After the pudding is prepared, pour it into the tart shell or shells, filling almost to the top of the crust. Arrange the strawberries, kiwifruit, and blueberries or blackberries attractively on top of the filling; cover and refrigerate for 2 hours. Release the tarts from the pan or pans and serve.

Decadent Chocolate Pudding

(UNDER 30 MINUTES)
SERVES 6

1½ cups organic
soft silken tofu

½ cup WestSoy Plus
vanilla soy milk

1 teaspoon umeboshi
pickled plum paste

9 tablespoons unprocessed
cocoa powder

6 tablespoons sugar

3 tablespoons unrefined
macadamia oil

1 teaspoon ground cinnamon

3 teaspoons cornstarch

1 teaspoon pure vanilla extract

Calories per serving: 219
Total fat: 9g
Saturated fat: 3g
Calories per serving from fat: 94
Protein: 7.5g
Carbohydrates: 27g
Dietary fiber: 4g
Sugars: 20g

If you crave chocolate, your urge will be satisfied without too much guilt by using unprocessed cocoa and unrefined macadamia oil, which is substituted for butter. Unprocessed cocoa contains fla-vanols (antioxidant compounds believed to be associated with potential cardiovascular benefits). Therefore, to reap the greatest benefits, buy unprocessed cocoa such as Navitas Naturals. Check at health-oriented grocery stores and online for this product; it is well worth the time. The umeboshi pickled plum paste creates a rich, delectable flavor.

Place ingredients in a blender, except for the vanilla, and blend until smooth. Frequently turn off the blender and scrape down the sides.

After it's blended, pour the mixture into a double boiler. Bring water to a boil over high heat; reduce heat to simmer and stir the mixture over simmering water for 5–7 minutes, or until the pud-ding has thickened. It will also become thicker after it cools.

Remove from heat, stir in the vanilla, and thoroughly mix. Pour into individual serving dishes. It may be served warm or cold. To serve cold, cover and refrigerate for 2 hours.

Calories per serving: 220
Total fat: 9g
Saturated fat: 3g
Calories from fat: 94
Protein: 7.5g
Carbohydrates: 27g
Dietary fiber: 4g
Sugars: 20g

Variation—Decadent Hot Chocolate Pudding

(UNDER 30 MINUTES)
SERVES 6

Chile and chocolate make an interesting and fiery combination. Follow the Decadent Chocolate Pudding recipe on page 172, but add 1–2 teaspoons of New Mexico red chile powder (mild, medium, or hot), and blend with the other ingredients.

Variation—Decadent Chocolate Espresso Pudding

(UNDER 30 MINUTES)
SERVES 6

Calories per serving: 221
Total fat: 9g
Saturated fat: 3g
Calories from fat: 94
Protein: 7.5g
Carbohydrates: 27g
Dietary fiber: 4g
Sugars: 20g

Coffee beans and chocolate are a wonderful combination. There may also be increased health benefits from adding coffee, which, like other plants, contains antioxidants—protectors against cancer, cardiovascular disease, and diabetes. Follow the Decadent Chocolate Pudding recipe on page 172, but blend in 1 or more teaspoons of finely ground espresso beans with the other ingredients. Use a spice grinder to achieve a powder-like consistency.

Lime Pudding with Fresh Raspberries

(UNDER 30 MINUTES)
SERVES 6

1 ½ **cups organic
silken tofu, soft or firm**

½ **cup Edensoy Extra Original
organic soy milk**

½ **teaspoon umeboshi
pickled plum paste**

½ **cup Key lime juice**

2 **teaspoons Key lime zest**

3 **tablespoons honey**

1 **tablespoon unrefined
macadamia oil**

3 **teaspoons cornstarch**

2 **teaspoons pure vanilla extract**

3 **cups raspberries**

2 **teaspoons minced mint leaves**

Calories per serving: 138
Total fat: 5g
Saturated fat: 0g
Calories from fat: 38
Protein: 5g
Carbohydrates: 22g
Dietary fiber: 3g
Sugars: 13g

Creamy lime pudding, without the fat that traditionally goes along with it, tastes delicious. One tablespoon of unrefined macadamia oil is added to achieve a creamy texture. High in monounsaturated fat and with a 1:1 Omega-6/Omega-3 EFA ratio, macadamia oil is good for you. Honey is used for flavor but can be replaced with sugar for children under 2. Warning: Children under 2 years of age should not eat raw or pasteurized honey. It may contain clostridium botulinum spores, which can germinate and cause botulism. The pasteurization temperature is not high enough to kill the spores in honey. Children over 2 can safely consume it, since the spores are toxic only in immature intestines.

Place all ingredients in a blender, except for the vanilla, raspberries, and mint; blend until smooth. Frequently turn off the blender and scrape down the sides.

Pour the mixture into a double boiler. Bring the water to a boil over high heat; reduce heat to low and stir the mixture over simmering water for approximately 5–7 minutes, or until the pudding has thickened. (It will continue to thicken as it cools.)

Remove from the heat, stir in the vanilla, and mix thoroughly. Allow to cool for about 20 minutes. Place ⅓ cup of raspberries in each individual serving dish and pour the pudding over the raspberries to completely cover. Top each serving with additional raspberries (I like to use 3 or 5) and some minced mint leaves

Cover and refrigerate for 2 hours.

Chocolate Fruit Parfait

(UNDER 30 MINUTES)
SERVES 6

1 cup raspberries

1 cup sliced bananas

1 cup blueberries

1 Decadent Chocolate Pudding
recipe (see page 172)

Calories per serving: 277
Total fat: 9g
Saturated fat: 3g
Calories from fat: 97
Protein: 8g
Carbohydrates: 42g
Dietary fiber: 4g
Sugars: 28g

A little bit of chocolate with a little bit of fruit creates a delightful combination.

Reserve 6 raspberries for garnish. Mix the remaining raspberries, bananas, and blueberries together; set aside. Prepare the pudding. Then fill four tall parfait glasses as follows: pour in a ¾-inch layer of pudding, followed by a similar amount of the fruit mixture. Repeat layers, ending with a layer of pudding, and top off each serving with a red raspberry. Cover and refrigerate for 2 hours.

Creamed Frozen Fruit Dessert

(UNDER 30 MINUTES)
SERVES 4

1 cup frozen mango cubes

1 cup frozen strawberries

½ cup Mori-Nu soft silken tofu, or non-silken firm tofu

1–2 cubes crystallized ginger, for sweetness (optional)

1 teaspoon Key lime zest

1 teaspoon pure vanilla extract

1 tablespoon unrefined macadamia oil (optional)

1 tablespoon frozen white grape juice concentrate or 1 tablespoon maple syrup, for sweetness (optional)

Calories per serving: 90
Total fat: 4g
Saturated fat: .5g
Calories from fat: 39
Protein: 2g
Carbohydrates: 12g
Dietary fiber: 2g
Sugars: 9g

Eat as you would sorbet, or spoon a dollop atop Summer Berry Crumble (see page 179) for an even yummier treat. If you desire the creaminess and taste of ice cream, add unrefined macadamia oil. You will be adding fat, but it is about 80 percent monounsaturated fat and has a heart-healthy 1:1 ratio of Omega-6/Omega-3 EFAs.

Allow the frozen mango and strawberries to soften slightly for 15 minutes. Place the tofu, ginger, lime zest, vanilla, and macadamia oil in a blender and blend until the ginger is blended with the other ingredients. Add half of the fruit mixture; blend. Add the reminder of the fruit and blend again until smooth. You may need to turn off the blender and stir occasionally.

Taste and adjust for sweetness by adding optional grape juice concentrate or maple syrup. Serve immediately as a very soft frozen dessert, or freeze for about 4 hours, then scoop out as you would a sorbet.

Crystallized ginger increases the calories by 8, carbohydrates by 2g, and sugars by 3g per serving.

White grape juice concentrate increases the calories by 11, carbohydrates by 9g, and sugars by 3g per serving.

Maple syrup increases calories by 11, carbohydrates by 3g, and sugars by 3g per serving.

Summer Berry Crumble

SERVES 6

4 cups mixed berries—
blueberries, blackberries, and
raspberries

1 cup sliced peaches

1 tablespoon Key lime juice

Zest from 1 Key lime

5 teaspoons sugar

⅛ teaspoon ground cardamom

4 teaspoons cornstarch

TOPPING

½ teaspoon butter or unrefined
macadamia oil

¾ cup rolled oats
(not instant or quick)

¼ cup quinoa flour

¼ cup organic golden flaxmeal

⅓ cup brown sugar

1 teaspoon ground cinnamon

¼ teaspoon nutmeg

¼ cup chopped pecans

½ teaspoon salt

3 tablespoons unrefined
macadamia oil

3 tablespoons butter

1 tablespoon maple syrup

Every time I bake a fresh berry crumble dessert, my mind races back to my childhood and picking blackberries, which my mother and I would turn into a cobbler or a crumble that very same day. Blackberries were plentiful throughout the area. Picking berries required walking; it was always a leisurely stroll, which involved visiting with family and friends during the pick. Our little trips often involved fishing (for catfish, perch, and bluegill) and picking berries. Crumbles are almost effortless to make. Since too much sugar takes away from the flavor of the fresh fruit (and adds extra pounds), this crumble is not heavily sweetened.

More than one seasonal fruit has been used to provide color and increase the healthy aspects of the recipe. Unrefined macadamia oil and flaxseed meal are used in place of some of the butter to reduce saturated fat and increase monounsaturated fat, along with improving the ratio of Omega-6/Omega-3 EFAs. I usually substitute macadamia oil for all of the butter, which creates a hint of nutty flavor.

Preheat the oven to 350 degrees F. In a large bowl, gently toss the mixed berries and peaches in lime juice and zest. Mix the sugar, cardamom, and cornstarch in a small bowl. Sprinkle this mixture over the fruit, and use a fork to gently toss until the fruit is coated. Allow to sit from 30 minutes to 1 hour at room temperature to absorb the sugar and bring out the flavors.

Select a shallow bowl or casserole dish, about 7–8 inches in diameter. Coat the bottom and sides with the ½ teaspoon of butter or macadamia oil. Place the fruit and its juices in the dish.

Calories per serving: 419
Total fat: 22g
Saturated fat: 5g
Calories from fat: 185
Protein: 8g
Carbohydrates: 53g
Dietary fiber: 11g
Sugars: 21g

Mix the oats, quinoa flour, flaxmeal, brown sugar, cinnamon, nutmeg, pecans, and salt together and set aside. Blend the macadamia oil and butter together with a fork until smooth. Using a pastry cutter or fork, cut the oil-butter mixture into the dry mixture until it resembles a coarse meal. Sprinkle this topping over the berries, covering completely. Drizzle maple syrup over the topping. Bake for about 45 minutes, or until bubbly and a little crusty on the sides.

Fruit Parfait

(UNDER 30 MINUTES)
SERVES 6

1 cup sliced strawberries

1 cup blueberries

1 cup sliced peaches

1 Creamed Frozen Fruit Dessert recipe (see page 177)

Organic golden flaxmeal and coarsely chopped pecans, for garnish

¼ cup blueberries, for garnish

6 whole strawberries, for garnish

Calories per serving: 105

Total fat: 4g

Saturated fat: <.5g

Calories from fat: 33

Protein: 2g

Carbohydrates: 17g

Dietary fiber: 3g

Sugars: 13g

Add taste-tempting appeal by layering parfait glasses with fruit and the Creamed Frozen Fruit Dessert on page 177. It's lighter, healthier fare than traditional ice cream fruit parfaits.

In a medium-size bowl, mix the strawberries, blueberries, and peaches together. Layer each parfait glass with alternating ¾-inch layers of the Frozen Fruit Dessert and the fruit mixture, starting and ending with a mound of the frozen dessert. Garnish with a sprinkling of flaxmeal and pecans, a few blueberries trickling down the mound, and a strawberry at the very top.

Highlights of Some Nutritional Studies

The Seven Countries Study

In the mid 1970s, research studies and scholarly articles about healthy foods and diets were not a mouse click away. Fortunately, I was a member of the Food Conspiracy, a health-oriented cooperative market in Tucson, where articles and chatter abounded regarding healthy foods and diets. Between the Food Conspiracy and the University of Arizona library, I gathered a lot of information to start building a healthy lifestyle and diet. Research is continually being done on foods or diets and how they impact our health. Today, valid research studies and scholarly articles are readily found via the Internet.

A study conducted in the mid-twentieth century prompted scientists to conduct more research to validate or to determine what made the Mediterranean and Japanese diets so healthy. In 1958, Ancel Keys (a researcher with a doctoral degree in physiology) began the Seven Countries Study, comparing diet, lifestyle, and the incidence of coronary heart disease among 12,700 middle-aged men from the United States, Japan, Italy, Greece, the Netherlands, Finland, and Yugoslavia. Heart disease was found to be rare in Greece, southern Italy, and Japan. The commonalities and mainstays of the Mediterranean and Japanese diets were a variety of fresh and cooked vegetables, whole grains, fruits, beans, and fish. Finland and the United States had the highest rate of heart disease. Red meat, cheese, and other foods high in saturated fats were prevalent in their diets.

The Seven Countries Study was the first study to successfully suggest a link between cardiovascular disease and risk factors with a variation in lifestyle and disease rates, prompting numerous clinical and laboratory studies on dietary fat and its effects on cardiovascular disease. Studies often isolated one or more elements of the Mediterranean diet to determine its effects on heart disease and other chronic diseases. Unfortunately, numerous fad diets and diet philosophies were born that didn't take the whole diet and lifestyle of the Mediterranean people into account. The Greeks in the 1960s were not a sedentary society. They also lived in a non-toxic environment, free of the pollutants that most populations have to deal with today.

Ancel Keys embraced the whole Mediterranean diet, led an active life, and lived to be 100 years old. Through books and articles he and his wife encouraged others to do the same. We followed his advice.

The Lyon Diet Heart Study

The Seven Countries Study showed that the people of Crete consumed large amounts of fat from olives, large amounts of plant foods, moderate amounts of fish and poultry, low amounts of meat, and moderate amounts of wine with meals. They experienced the longest life expectancy, compared with other populations, and had very low rates of cardiovascular disease and certain cancers. Started in 1988, the Lyon Heart Study was the first clinical examination of the health benefits of the Mediterranean diet. Over six hundred patients, all of whom who had previously had one heart attack, either followed a Mediterranean diet or the American Heart Association Step I diet, which limited total fat to 30 percent and saturated fat to 10 percent. Originally intended to last five years, for ethical reasons the study was stopped after two years. The study showed that patients following the Mediterranean diet (reducing their Omega-6 EFA intake) had a significantly lower risk of recurrent heart disease and fatal heart attack.

Adherence to a Mediterranean Diet and Survival in a Greek Population

Between 1994 and 1999, 22,043 participants who ranged in age from 20 to 86 were enrolled in the Greek component of the European Prospective Investigation into Cancer and Nutrition

(EPIC). The researchers concluded that there is an association between greater adherence to the traditional Mediterranean diet and a reduction in total mortality, as well as a reduction in death from both coronary heart disease and cancer. The researchers suggested that the study confirms the effects of a high ratio of monounsaturated fat to saturated fat in the reduction of mortality.

The Washington Heights-Inwood Columbia Aging Project

This study, published in the spring of 2006, was the first to consider the whole diet of individuals, based on the Mediterranean diet, and draw conclusions about diet and disease. When the study began, it was composed of 2,258 non-demented, community-based individuals in their seventies. During this four-year study, 272 individuals were diagnosed with Alzheimer's. The study showed that the higher the adherence to a Mediterranean-type diet, the lower the risk of developing Alzheimer's. Research also indicated a link between the Mediterranean diet and lower vascular risks such as hypertension, bad cholesterol levels, and diabetes. Dr. Nikolaos Scarmeas, who headed the study, stated that more studies replicating this study need to be done to increase the confidence levels.

Okinawa Centenarian Study

Okinawa has one of the world's highest concentrations of centenarians. Starting in 1976 and spanning more than thirty years, over 800 Okinawan centenarians, along with numerous individuals in their seventies, eighties, and nineties, were interviewed and examined. The majority of Okinawan elders enjoy a high quality of life marked by lucid minds and a low rate of lifestyle-related illnesses such as cardiovascular disease, cancer, diabetes, osteoporosis, dementia, and Alzheimer's disease. In addition, the women are pretty much free of the ills of menopause. Head research team members Makoto Suzuki, Dr. Bradley Willcox, and Dr. Craig Willcox attribute this phenomenon of healthy aging and longevity to a number of combined factors. They suggest that genes play a role in longevity and healthy aging, but that lifestyle also has a significant impact. The elderly Okinawans get plenty of physical and mental exercise by practicing martial arts, dancing, gardening, walking, and bicycling. They have strong social bonds within their community and practice an easygoing philosophy. Their diets are low in calories, with a low glycemic load, and Okinawans practice the dietary philosophy known as *hara hachi bu*—to stop eating when they are 80 percent satisfied. Their diets are high in fruits, vegetables, and whole grains, low in red meat consumption, and low in fat. They consume alcohol in moderation, eat three servings of fish high in Omega-3 fatty acids each week, and consume more soy than any other culture, mostly in the form of tofu and edamame. Okinawans who have moved from Okinawa and are following the lifestyles of their new surroundings are experiencing dramatically higher rates of cancer and heart disease.

Food, Nutrition and the Prevention of Cancer

During my quest for beneficial dietary knowledge, I came across *Food, Nutrition and the Prevention of Cancer: A Global Perspective.* This report was forged from a four-year project commissioned by the executive officers of the World Cancer Research Fund and the American Institute for Cancer Research. In 2007, WCRF/AICR is publishing the second expert report, including a review and evaluation of an estimated 10,000 pieces of research on diet, physical activity, and weight management and their effect on cancer risk, so some of these guidelines may change.

The expert report published in the fall of 1997 is considered by the AICR to be the most comprehensive report to date in the field of diet and cancer. The research panel estimates that between 30 and 40 percent of cancer cases worldwide are preventable through dietary means, based on an assessment of over 4,500 research studies linking foods, nutrition, food preparation, dietary patterns, and related factors. The panel formulated the following life-saving recommendations:

1. Choose a predominantly plant-based diet rich in a variety of vegetables and fruits, legumes, and minimally processed starchy staple foods. (This does not imply that a vegetarian diet is more protective against cancer than diets that may include many protective foods along with a modest amount of meat.)

2. Avoid being underweight or overweight, and limit weight gain during adulthood to less than eleven pounds.

3. If occupational activity is low or moderate, take an hour-long brisk walk or similar aerobic exercise daily (the report also recommends an additional hour of more vigorous exercise once a week).

4. Eat 400–800 grams (15–30 ounces) or five or more portions a day of a variety of vegetables and fruits providing 7 percent or more of total calories, all year round (not including legumes and starchy vegetables and fruits—tubers, starchy roots, and plantains). The evidence of protection from cancer is strongest for green vegetables, raw vegetables, the onion family, carrots, tomatoes, and citrus fruit. Many fruits and vegetables contain fiber, carotenoids, vitamin C, and many other bioactive compounds. The protective benefits of fruits and vegetables may be short-lived in the body, so these nutrients need to be replenished daily.

5. Eat 600–800 grams (20–30 ounces) or more than seven portions a day of a variety of cereals (grains), legumes, roots, tubers, and plantains (yams, bananas, etc.), providing 45–60 percent of total calories. These foods are good sources of folate (folic acid), carotenoids, and vitamin C. Eat a minimum amount of processed foods and limit the consumption of refined sugar to less than 10 percent of total calories.

6. Alcohol consumption is not recommended; pregnant women, women at risk of breast cancer, children, and adolescents should

not drink alcohol. If consumed at all, limit alcoholic drinks to less than 2 drinks a day for men and 1 for women. A drink is defined as one small glass of beer, one glass of wine, or a shot of spirits.

7. If eaten at all, limit intake of red meat (beef, lamb, and pork, and products made from these meats) to less than 80 grams (3 ounces) daily. Meat should provide less than 10 percent of total calories, and it is preferable to choose fish, poultry, or meat from non-domesticated animals. Diets containing substantial amounts of red meat and/or animal fat probably increase the risk of cancers of the colon and rectum, and possibly pancreas, breast, prostate, lung, endometrium, and kidney cancers as well. Substantial amounts of grilled, broiled, or well-cooked meat and fish may increase the risk of stomach cancer, and cancers of the colon and rectum may be increased by substantial amounts of grilled, broiled, barbecued, or fried meats.

8. Limit consumption of fatty foods, particularly those of animal origin. Total fats and oils should provide 15 percent to no more than 30 percent of total calories. Choose modest amounts of appropriate vegetable oils. Vegetable oils should be predominantly monounsaturated, such as olive oil, with minimum hydrogenation. (Note: Since this report, evidence based on research has surfaced that shows low-fat diets may not be the healthiest. What is important is the type of fat that is consumed—saturated fat should be held to 10 percent, no hydrogenated oils should be consumed, and predominantly monounsaturated fats should be consumed.)

9. Limit consumption of salted foods and use of cooking and table salt to less than 6 g (1 teaspoon) for adults per day. Children should consume no more than 3g or ½ teaspoon per day for a diet of 1,000 calories. Use herbs and spices to season foods. Manufactured foods and salt-cured foods have high salt content.

The risk of stomach cancer is possibly increased by diets high in salted foods.

10. Store perishable food in ways that minimize fungal contamination (this guideline pertains mostly to grain storage by food suppliers). Do not eat food that, as a result of long storage at ambient temperatures, is liable to contamination with mycotoxins.

11. Perishable food, if not consumed promptly, needs to be refrigerated or frozen.

12. When levels of additives, contaminants, and other residues are properly regulated, their presence in food and drink is not known to be harmful. However, unregulated or improper use can be a health hazard, particularly in economically developing countries.

13. Do not eat charred food. Meat and fish eaters should avoid burning meat juices. Consume meat and fish grilled (broiled) in direct flame, and cured and smoked meats, only occasionally.

14. For those who follow the recommendations presented here, dietary supplements are probably unnecessary, and possibly unhelpful, for reducing cancer risk.

15. Do not smoke or chew tobacco.

It is important to note that the longer these recommendations are practiced, the more protection you have. What you do from today on will have an impact on your health and your family's health for decades to come.

Anti-Inflammatory Diet

Respected nutritional experts, including Andrew Weil, M.D., are recommending anti-inflammatory diets, which are essentially based on the Mediterranean diet. Anti-inflammatory diets recommend an increase in consumption of **Omega**-3 EFAs in order to achieve a better Omega-6/Omega-3 ratio (see page 202 for more on EFAs) and include other dietary recommendations to put the body into an anti-inflammatory state. Basic guidelines include eating wild cold-water fish, replacing high-Omega-6 oils with extra-virgin olive oil, eating an abundance of colorful nutrient-rich fresh fruits and vegetables and whole grains, limiting foods with a high glycemic load, eating less animal protein and replacing it with vegetable protein as much as possible, eliminating or minimizing processed and fast foods, limiting consumption of saturated fats and trans fats, and avoiding over-eating.

The theory of abnormal inflammation in the body is in relation to the level of C-reactive protein (CRP) in the blood. It is believed that CRP rises with increased levels of inflammation and that slight elevations of CRP increase the risk for a number of chronic diseases, such as heart attack, stroke, and Alzheimer's disease. If you think you are at risk, a physician can order a blood test to measure CRP. A growing body of evidence suggests that consumption of Omega-3 is your best bet for reducing the level of CRP in the blood. When Omega-6 to Omega-3 consumption is in balance, inflammation is kept at bay and CRP is reduced in the blood. When it is lopsided, with substantially more Omega-6 than Omega-3, inflammation occurs and an increase in CRP results.

Andrew Weil explains abnormal inflammation in the body and its negative affects on health in his book *Healthy Aging*. He further explains how diet can influence inflammation and recommends dietary guidelines. Another resource for more information about the anti-inflammatory diet is Barry Sears, who has written *The Anti-Inflammation Zone* and is president of the nonprofit Inflammation Research Foundation (www.inflammationresearchfoundation.org). Both books are like bibles for those interested in maintaining a healthy mind and body into advanced age, and I have taken their recommendations to heart in writing *The Healthy Southwest Table*. You can enjoy the tastes of the Southwest offered in this recipe book while following the guidelines provided by both Weil and Sears.

A Healthier Lifestyle

Many chronic conditions are diseases of lifestyle. They don't suddenly occur but develop, unnoticed, over a period of years. By making healthy lifestyle choices, you can significantly reduce the odds of succumbing to one or more of these diseases in the future.

According to the Centers for Disease Control's 2003–2004 National Health and Nutrition Examination Survey, 34 percent of adults in the U.S. are overweight, and an additional 32 percent suffer from obesity, which poses serious health issues. The number of overweight adults almost doubled from 1980 to 1999. Since the 1970s, overweight levels have tripled among adolescents and more than doubled among younger children. The increased consumption of fast foods, processed foods, bad fats, and simple carbohydrates, and the lack of a variety of vegetables in daily diets, along with increasingly sedentary lifestyles, are contributors to this increase in an overweight population. Such an unhealthy lifestyle is the foundation for an increased risk in later years for heart disease, various cancers, diabetes, and other chronic diseases.

The lifestyle choice of whether or not to exercise is more important today than ever before. With individuals relying on motorized transportation rather than walking or biking, and the popularity of personal computers, TV, and video games, many people's lifestyles have become inordinately sedentary. A lifestyle without exercise puts people at a higher risk for cardiovascular disease, osteoporosis, and certain cancers. Diet and exercise are the two aspects of your life that are under your control and can reduce the risk of many chronic diseases.

Since our children were small we have hiked, biked, strolled, and snow-skied together. All four children were involved in sports, and Blake and Amanda played soccer and volleyball, respectively, throughout college. They continue to play on teams a couple of times per week and jog. Alex plays golf. Whenever we all get together, we play softball and hike in Sabino Canyon. My husband and I walk, and I also do Pilates.

Making Smart Food Choices

Fruits and Vegetables: Colorful Defenders against Disease

The cells in your body use oxygen to produce energy, but in the process your body produces toxic substances called free radicals, which damage the structure of your cells. Antioxidant enzymes in your body naturally take care of the free radicals. Combining an unhealthy diet and an industrialized environment full of pollutants and stress puts our bodies into oxidative overload that the body's natural antioxidant enzymes cannot handle. As a result of the damage from free radicals, your body may succumb to disease.

Don't worry; you are not doomed! You have a shot at changing your fate by consuming a variety of foods containing potent antioxidant substances that can reduce the amount of free radicals in your body. These free radical avengers are in foods containing carotenoid compounds and vitamins C and E.

Cruciferous vegetables (so named due to the cross or crucifix shape of their flower petals) are abundant in carotenoids, aiding in the detoxification of free radicals in our cells and in eliminating them from the body. Broccoli, bok choy, brussels sprouts, cabbage, collards, kale, chard, radishes, and turnips are in the cruciferous vegetable family. The deep, rich color of a vegetable indicates its antioxidant strength. Broccoli florets are on the top of the list of foods containing cancer-fighting antioxidants. Broccoli is also high in vitamin C and fiber.

To ensure your body has the best defense, consume a large variety of fruits and vegetables, which will help you obtain the full spectrum of antioxidants and nutrients. There are over 500 carotenoid compounds and other disease-preventive phytochemicals that work to block the development of cancer and other diseases. In addition to the cruciferous vegetables, deeply colored produce such as red tomatoes, red bell peppers, carrots, sweet potatoes, winter squash, spinach, beet greens, parsley, cilantro, eggplant (unpeeled), strawberries, raspberries, red and purple grapes, blueberries, tangerines, oranges, red grapefruit, mangoes, apricots, cantaloupe, and papaya are excellent sources of phytochemicals. When you shop for produce, buy a wide variety. Mix purples, oranges, yellows, reds, greens, whites, and browns. Buy vegetables, fruits, and mushrooms. Add color!

Vitamin C is plentiful in citrus fruits, tomatoes (pasta sauce and salsa), strawberries, kiwis, peppers, broccoli, and cauliflower. Whole grains and fatty foods—natural vegetable oils, nuts, and seeds—are the best sources of vitamin E. Vitamins C and E and the phytochemicals work together as a team to combat cancer and other diseases; this team has to be available to your body daily.

There is convincing evidence that the allium vegetables— onions, shallots, leeks, chives, and garlic—protect against stomach and colon cancers, and are heart-healthy. Among the onions, ordinary yellow onions give the most protection. It is believed that organosulfides, the substances in onions that makes us cry, help our bodies convert toxic chemicals into harmless by-products rather than into carcinogens. They are most protective when eaten raw; the pesto sauces, salsas, and pasta salad recipes in this book are wonderful sources for raw alliums.

Have you ever heard that red wine can reduce the risk of heart disease? Phenolics (antioxidant compounds) in the wine are responsible for its heart-healthy attributes. But according to the American Institute for Cancer Research, women at high risk for breast cancer should not consume any alcohol. You can benefit from the same heart-protective compound found in red wine by eating sun-dried raisins, which contain significant levels of phenolics. With sun-dried raisins, people of all ages can enjoy the benefits phenolics provide, year-round.

The fiber and tartaric acid in raisins also keep the colon healthy by efficiently ridding it of waste. Raisins and grapes are the only common foods that contain tartaric acid. Red and purple grapes, with their deep color, provide rich sources of cancer and disease-fighting substances. Next time you pack a lunch, pack grapes.

The American Institute for Cancer Research recommends that you consume five servings of a variety of fruits and vegetables and an additional seven servings of root vegetables and tubers each day. (For complete recommendations, see page 185.)

The Importance of Folate (Folic Acid)

People of all ages need folate in their diets. It is believed to reduce the risk of heart attacks, strokes, some cancers, osteoporosis, and Alzheimer's disease, and it is known to prevent fetal growth defects.

Due to overwhelming evidence that insufficient folate in the mother's diet can cause abnormalities of an unborn child's brain and spinal cord, such as spina bifida, the U.S. Public Health Service recommends that all women of childbearing age, whether or not they are pregnant, consume 400 micrograms (mcg) of folic acid per day. This is because neural tube abnormalities occur during the first 12 weeks of pregnancy, often before prenatal vitamins (which contain folic acid) are prescribed.

Among the elderly, Alzheimer's disease is the leading cause of dementia. Studies have shown that higher blood levels of the amino acid homocysteine, produced when the body breaks down protein, may increase the risk of developing Alzheimer's disease and other types of dementia. Animal protein produces more homocysteine than plant protein. Fortunately, folic acid transforms homocysteine into a harmless byproduct. A number of studies published since 2000 indicate that higher levels of folate through diet and supplements may offer protection against Alzheimer's. A number of studies currently under way should further determine if there is an association between folate and other B vitamins and Alzheimer's disease.

Homocysteine may also prove to be a major risk for the heart. Higher than normal levels of homocysteine in the blood correspond to an increased chance of blood vessel damage and increased potential for cholesterol buildup in the bloodstream, which sets the stage for blockages in the arteries. The Kuopio Ischemic Heart Disease Risk Factor Study, published in 2001, found that the 980 men in the ten-year study who consumed the most dietary folate had about half the risk of an acute coronary event, compared with those who consumed the least dietary folate. Since researchers are not certain if the increase in folic acid intake is a factor in decreasing rates of cardiovascular disease, several clinical studies are under way.

The bottom line: Substitute some plant protein for animal protein to reduce the production of homocysteine. Recipes from *The Healthy Southwest Table* are high in plant protein, and many of the recipes contain citrus fruits, tomatoes, avocados, beans, whole grains, asparagus, and leafy green vegetables such as spinach, broccoli, and chard, all of which are good sources of folic acid. Cooked vegetables lose about half of their folate value. Therefore, it is important to eat fresh fruits and uncooked vegetables. Four cups of fresh spinach supply 400 mcg of folate. Also, legumes are a good source of folate—½ cup of garbanzo beans will provide 140 mcg and ½ cup of lentils, 180 mcg. To increase your folate intake, hummus (pages 58–63) is a great option, accompanied by fresh vegetables for dipping.

Carbohydrates and Glycemic Load

Carbohydrates are an extremely important part of a health-oriented diet. They provide the fuel necessary for physical activity and organ function, along with valuable fiber, phytonutrients, vitamins, and minerals. When digested, carbohydrates break down into sugar, which enters the bloodstream and raises the level of blood sugar. Insulin is produced, triggering cell receptors to receive the sugar, which is stored in the body's cells or burned

for energy. However, different carbohydrate foods have different effects on blood sugar.

The best choices of carbohydrate foods are those that are slow to digest, in order to maintain a slow, even rise in blood sugar and insulin secretion. Carbs in foods that are digested very rapidly, such as white bread, cause a spike in blood sugar and a greater demand of insulin secretion to regulate the blood sugar level, which in a couple of hours may also cause a sharp decrease in blood sugar levels. Over time, a continuous spiking of blood sugar over-burdens the cells in the pancreas that produce insulin. They may wear out and eventually stop working.

Carbs to eliminate or reduce in your diet are white and refined whole wheat breads, white rice, quick oats, white potatoes, all kinds of chips, pastries, soda, junk food in general, and foods containing high-fructose corn syrup. Instead choose moderate servings of starches high in fiber, such as coarse whole-grain breads and cereals, brown rice, beans, whole-grain pasta cooked "al dente," yams, carrots, and generous servings of high-fiber fruits and vegetables such as apricots, berries, asparagus, green beans, broccoli, and cauliflower. A good reference regarding favorable and unfavorable carbs is *The Anti-Inflammation Zone* by Barry Sears.

Many variables affect the rate at which a carbohydrate is digested and the rise in blood sugar. For example, if you eat a combination of protein, fat, and carbohydrate, the fat and protein slow down the digestion of the carbohydrate and, thus, blood sugar is raised slowly. The riper a banana, the faster it turns to sugar; cooked vegetables and grains convert to sugar faster than uncooked. If an acid—red or white wine vinegar, apple cider vinegar, lemon, or lime—is present, carbohydrate digestion is slowed down. Also, sourdough bread slows down digestion, as do pickled products.

If you become familiar with the glycemic load (GL) of foods, you can make healthy carbohydrate choices and serving sizes. The GL ranking system is based on the amount of available carbohydrate in a standard serving size of a particular food. The GL takes into consideration the quality of a carbohydrate and the quantity per serving. A GL under 10 is low, 11–15 is medium, and over 20 is high. A total GL per day less than 80 is low and over 120 is high. You can retrieve GLs of foods (including brand-name foods) from the University of Sydney at www.glycemicindex.com.

A piece of soft commercial white bread has a GL of 10, while a coarse seven-whole-grain piece of bread has a GL of 5. Many whole-grain breads are heavily processed, producing a soft whole-grain product, which will have a higher GL number. The coarser the grain the longer it takes to digest. What is important is the total GL of a meal, which is affected by the combination of fat, protein, fiber, degree of cooking, uncooked grains, vegetables, and so on.

Consistently eating snacks and meals with a high GL increases serum triglyceride levels and decreases the "good cholesterol," HDL, both of which are associated with an increased risk of cardiovascular disease. Such a diet is also associated with increasing the serum levels of C-reactive protein (CRP) that increases during systemic inflammation, which also indicates a higher risk of cardiovascular disease and Alzheimer's disease. There is also a higher risk of obesity and diabetes mellitus type 2 and cancer.

Can the Right Fats Make You Healthy?

Since the early 1990s, there has been so much ado about limiting fat in the diet that the importance and benefits of some fats may be overlooked. It is important not to indiscriminately reduce fat; instead, we should be "fat wise" by selectively eliminating the bad fats and replacing them with health-promoting fats.

REDUCE SATURATED FAT. Throughout the twentieth century, studies have shown that people in countries where the diet includes large amounts of meat and whole-milk dairy products have higher rates of heart disease and cancer than people in other countries. (This diet high in saturated fat is fairly typical for the United States.) Saturated fat takes its toll on our cardiovascular systems by raising the levels of both triglycerides and LDL cholesterol in the blood. High levels of triglycerides and LDL (often referred to as "bad" cholesterol) increase the risk of fatty deposits, causing a narrowing of the arteries (artherosclerosis), which restricts blood flow and makes the vessels less elastic. This results in a higher risk for a heart attack or debilitating stroke.

Most cardiovascular disease is very preventable. This lifestyle disease does not develop overnight, and even if hereditary factors cause individuals to be prone to dangerous cholesterol levels, dietary intervention can improve the LDL cholesterol and triglyceride levels in the blood. However, sometimes a combination of medication, diet, and exercise is the only alternative.

High consumption of saturated fat increases inflammation, which is associated with heart disease, cancer, Alzheimer's disease, type 2 diabetes mellitus, and other chronic diseases. High saturated fat consumption also causes obesity, which in turn is linked to cancer, diabetes, high blood pressure, and many other health problems. For example, the Nurses' Health Study II (established in 1989 by organizations from the Massachusetts medical community) concluded that young-adult women who consume large amounts of red meat and high-fat dairy foods are at increased risk for breast cancer. Food, Nutrition, and the Prevention of Cancer: A Global Perspective was a research project funded by the American Institute for Cancer Research and the World Cancer Research Fund, with results published in 1997. Its findings indicate that the incidence of cancer could be reduced worldwide by 30 to 40 percent through proper diet, exercise, and weight control. This report recommends that if eaten at all, only three ounces of red meat—beef, lamb, or pork—should be consumed each day. To attain this goal, red meat could be replaced with poultry, fish, or meat from non-domesticated animals. The Food, Nutrition, and the Prevention of Cancer report also advises that meatless diets are compatible with good health and low cancer risk. In addition, it recommends that fatty foods from animal sources, such as butter and lard, be replaced with monounsaturated oils such as olive oil.

AVOID TROPICAL AND HYDROGENATED OILS AND FATS. The American diet is not only filled with saturated fats derived from animal sources, but is also loaded with hydrogenated oils and tropical oils—coconut oil, palm oil, and palm kernel oil (all of which are mostly saturated fat). One danger of hydrogenated oils stems from the trans fatty acids (TFAs, also called trans fats) lurking in these oils. Research studies suggest that TFAs could prove even worse for our cardiovascular system than animal fat. TFAs are byproducts of converting vegetable oils—canola oil, corn oil, soybean oil, etc.—from their natural fluid state to a more stable solid or semi-solid state through the process of hydrogenation. TFAs not only add hardness to fat, but they can also harden your arteries. So when you see hydrogenated or partially hydrogenated canola oil in foods, it is no longer the health-promoting monounsaturated oil that it once was.

In April 2006, a review article in the *New England Journal of Medicine* reported on findings from the Harvard School of Public Health and Wageningen University about the health hazards of TFAs, based on evidence from numerous studies. TFAs have negative effects on blood lipids—raising LDL and triglycerides, and decreasing HDL (or "good" cholesterol); TFAs promote inflammation and cause blood-vessel abnormalities, all of which are associated with higher rates of cardiovascular disease and diabetes mellitus type 2. Based on a combined analysis of a number of studies, the research found that a diet with as little as 2 percent of calories consumed from TFAs increased the risk of coronary heart disease by 23 percent. Just as an example, a medium serving of fast-food French fries would account for 40 calories from TFAs—this would be 2 percent of a daily intake of 2,000 calories.

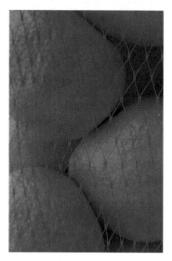

Since the majority of people who consume hydrogenated and tropical oils on a regular basis are unaware of their dangers, they are silent killers. Once you start reading labels, you will be amazed at the products you use every day that contain these potentially harmful substances. One friend who was trying to reduce saturated fat in her family's diet bought low-fat whole-grain breads, cereals, and other whole-grain packaged foods—but all of the products contained hydrogenated oil. She didn't realize that hydrogenated canola oil was different from regular canola oil. These oils are used in many of our favorite foods and convenience foods. Do you like crispy, fried chicken? Vegetable shortening (hydrogenated fat) is used to achieve that crispiness. Hydrogenated vegetable shortening also gives body to cake frosting and a chewy texture to cookies.

Take a look at the foods in your home and see how much saturated fat you are consuming on a daily basis under the names of hydrogenated or partially hydrogenated oil. You will find hydrogenated or tropical oils in many breads and other baked goods, most candies, desserts, puddings, crackers, almost all major cereal brands, soups, non-dairy creamers, processed meat, many prepared foods, and fast foods. Major packaged food manufacturers continue to misrepresent whole-grain cereals and whole-grain breads as health foods even though they contain hydrogenated oils. They are even added to peanut butter to make it creamy. Try finding low-fat microwave popcorn without hydrogenated oil.

Dairy cases in grocery stores are filled with margarine claiming to be better than butter. Yet compared with butter, it puts us at even greater risk for heart attack or stroke, because hiding in margarine are those trans fatty acids from hydrogenated oils. Try spreading avocado on your bread instead of butter and reap the benefits derived from a whole, fresh food loaded with mono-unsaturated fat, vitamin E, and fiber. Or spray olive oil on bread and benefit from the healthy values of monounsaturated fat.

Packaging or advertising often is misleading, so read the labels. Beware! Just as you can't judge a book by its cover, you can't judge a food by its package. A close friend of mine went to the grocery store, and upon her return home her husband asked where she had been so long. She replied, "Reading labels, and we are in big trouble."

In December 2006, New York City's Board of Health banned the use of TFAs in New York City restaurants. The mayor commented that he loved hamburgers and French fries and that the board's purpose was not to take them away from New Yorkers but to request that restaurants make them with less-damaging ingredients. Prominent national chains, including Starbucks, Taco Bell, KFC, Burger King, Arby's, and McDonald's, are also joining the trend toward eliminating TFAs from their menus. If you eat at these establishments, you can check their websites periodically to review nutritional information and find out what they are using to replace the TFAs.

MONOUNSATURATED AND POLYUNSATURATED FATS: GOOD FAT. Low-fat diets are of little benefit in losing weight and may actually be hazardous to your health. If you eliminate too many of the good fats, you might increase your risk for cardiovascular disease, cancer, arthritis, and osteoporosis, to mention just a few. In 1993, the Women's Health Initiative Dietary Modification Trial (a nationwide study based in Bethesda, Maryland) began. Forty percent of the 50,000 participants followed a low-fat diet, while 60 percent followed their regular diets. After eight years, researchers noted no apparent gain in protection against cardiovascular disease or breast or colorectal cancer, and weights remained about the same as at the beginning of the study. However, there was evidence to suggest that replacing saturated fats and trans fats with polyunsaturated and monounsaturated fats could effectively reduce the risk of heart disease and some cancers. Along these same lines, the Nurses' Health Study, which started in 1976 and has continued into the twenty-first century, has shown that heart disease risk was lowered by about 30 to 40 percent by replacing 80 calories of carbohydrates with 80 calories of either polyunsaturated or monounsaturated fats. Food sources for these "good" fats include nuts, freshly ground flaxmeal, olives, and fatty coldwater fish.

This takes us right back to the Seven Countries Study and the Mediterranean diet. The right fat is indeed healthy, as evidenced by the traditional diets of the people residing in the Mediterranean area, who had low rates of cardiovascular and other chronic diseases. This low incidence of disease may be partially due to the consumption of large amounts of olive oil and olives, which contain monounsaturated fats. Olives also contain many antioxidants that help to keep the body in a healthy state.

Unlike saturated fats, polyunsaturated and monounsaturated fats do not raise the level of LDL cholesterol in the blood. In fact, evidence from the Nurses' Study suggests that in consuming these fats, LDL cholesterol levels in the blood are lowered, while HDL levels are maintained or slightly raised. Monounsaturated fats further reduce the risk of heart attack by lowering the level of triglycerides in the blood. (On the other hand, polyunsaturated fats, such as safflower and corn oil, tend to lower both LDL *and* HDL cholesterol, but you want to maintain a high HDL level in the blood to reduce the risk of cardiovascular disease. Because of this, I actually prefer to use monounsaturated fats almost exclusively.)

ESSENTIAL FATTY ACIDS (EFAs): GOOD FAT. Our bodies do not produce essential fatty acids (EFAs); these are obtained only through the foods we eat. Just as their name implies, we need them, but in our quest to reduce overall fat, we may eliminate or reduce the essential ones from our diets. Among the better-known EFAs are Omega-3 and Omega-6. Extensive research indicates that Omega-3 EFAs reduce inflammation and reduce the risk of chronic diseases such as heart disease, cancer, and arthritis. There is also strong evidence that Omega-3 EFAs may reduce dementia and help alleviate depression. Omega-6 is essential for healthy hair, skin, bones, and more, although it is easy to get too much of it, which can be detrimental.

Cold, deep-water, fatty fish—salmon, fresh tuna, herring, mackerel, anchovies, and sardines—are excellent sources of two Omega-3 fatty acids, eicosapentenoic acid (EPA) and docosahexenoic acid (DHA). The Cardiovascular Health Cognition Study (conducted in the 1990s by the University of Pittsburgh's Department of Neurology) found strong evidence that eating fatty fish is associated with lower risk of dementia and Alzheimer's disease (which is believed to be associated with inflammation) for those individuals who are not carriers of the apolipoprotein e4 gene (a gene associated with a greater risk of getting Alzheimer's).

The American Heart Association recommends that these heart-friendly fish be included twice each week in an overall low-fat diet, although you should bake fish at no more than 350 degrees F to preserve the Omega-3 health-promoting values in the fish. (Treat yourself to one of the delicious salmon or sable fish recipes in *The Healthy Southwest Table,* which help shield you from disease.) In the October 2006 issue of *JAMA (Journal of the American Medical Association),* Dr. Dariush Mozaffarian and fellow researcher Eric Rimm present evidence that eating six ounces per week of fatty (dark meat) fish high in Omega-3 EFAs may reduce the risk of dying from heart disease by 36 percent and reduce total mortality by 17 percent.

Flaxseeds are an excellent source of plant-based Omega-3 EFAs, provided they are sufficiently ground up. Grind the seeds into meal and include four tablespoons of flaxmeal in your diet daily for the greatest benefit. Once the seed is ground, store it in an airtight container in the refrigerator to preserve the Omega-3 EFAs and vitamin E. *The Healthy Southwest Table* includes flaxmeal in many recipes. Since flax loses its Omega-3 EFA benefits at high temperatures, it too should be baked at no more than 350 degrees F. An even better option is to sprinkle the flax over recipes that have been cooked, or add it to salads.

It is believed that humans evolved on a diet with a ratio of Omega-6 EFAs to Omega-3 EFAs of 1:1. In the United States today, the average ratio is about 17:1, with a common range anywhere from 10:1 to 50:1. This is due to a diet high in junk foods, packaged, canned, and processed foods, and fast foods. The oils used in most of these foods are corn, sunflower, soy, safflower, cottonseed, or canola. Most of these oils are highly processed and hydrogenated, and with the exception of canola oil, they are high in Omega-6 EFAs with little or no Omega-3 EFAs. By ingesting foods with these oils, the Omega-6/Omega-3 ratio becomes dangerously out of balance.

Omega-3 EFAs are likely to reduce inflammation, while Omega-6 EFAs tend to promote inflammation. Balanced EFAs also play an important part in defense against cancer. If there is not a healthy balance, it is believed that the body's immune system is weakened. Also, there is evidence that consuming a higher ratio of Omega-6 to Omega-3 can promote tumor growth. So, shoot for that almost impossible ratio of 1:1.

Due to the amount of pesticides in cottonseed oil, stay clear of any foods containing it. Also, since rapeseeds, from which canola oil is made, are heavily sprayed with pesticides, buy only organic, and look for cold-pressed, unrefined canola oil, which has all the health benefits intact. It is available mostly in health-oriented grocery stores and health food stores. Interestingly, the more Omega-3 EFAs in an oil, the less desirable it is for cooking. Heat not only eliminates the healthy properties of the oil but can change it into dangerous TFAs. Therefore, flax oil, which is high in Omega-3, should never be used for sautéing. This also holds true for unrefined canola oil. Macadamia oil is high in unsaturated fat and has a 1:1 ratio of

Omega-6 to Omega 3. I suggest using it in baking instead of butter, using temperatures of 350 degrees F or less.

The moral of the EFAs saga is to eat foods high in Omega-3 EFAs—small wild Alaskan salmon, wild sable fish, and flaxseed—for healthy arteries and to limit the production of cancer-producing elements inherent in Omega-6 EFAs. If you eat foods rich in Omega-3s and consume foods high in mono-unsaturated fats—olives, olive oil, avocado, unrefined macadamia oil, and flaxmeal—you are automatically going to get enough Omega-6.

Acknowledgments

I want to thank Dominic Wallen for encouraging me; without his support and belief in me, this book would have never been written. A huge "thank you" goes to John Heider, who carried my idea to the publisher. A special thanks goes to my daughter, Elicia Kniffin, who tested all of the recipes in the book and was always there to critique the recipes, join in recipe debate, and look over the manuscript with a discerning eye. I am so grateful to my mother, Leone Witt, who taught me to cook from scratch, using fresh ingredients. Many thanks go to Lloyd and Carol Smith, Alice Udall, Carrie Montesano (who proofed and offered valuable suggestions), and to Gloria Taylor, Jessie De La Ossa, Claudia Pena, Victoria Taylor, Dara De La Ossa, Christina Brito, and Laura Udall for the time they spent faithfully testing the recipes and providing me with invaluable feedback. I am grateful for my editors Carrie Stusse and Lisa Cooper, who kept prodding me for clarification until they were satisfied with the final draft. Last, but certainly not least, a warm thanks to Tracy Vega, who keeps me in her heart in promoting my work.

For More Information

Weil, Andrew. *Healthy Aging: A Lifelong Guide to Your Physical and Spiritual Well-Being.* New York: Alfred A. Knopf, 2005.

Sears, Barry. *The Anti-Inflammation Zone: Reversing the Silent Epidemic That's Destroying Our Health.* New York: Regan Books/Harper Collins, 2005.

The World's Healthiest Foods, http://whfoods.org

www.drweil.com

Index